MY CRIME SERIES - THE FIRST OFFENSE

FIVE TRUE CRIME STORIES FROM CALIFORNIA INMATES

EAST OAKLAND TIMES, LLC

MY CRIME SERIES

The books of the My Crime series are neither meant to justify nor condemn the inmates on whom they are written. Rather, the books of the My Crime series propose to candidly communicate the upbringing, life experience, and motivations of the incarcerated.

The My Crime series puts you as the judge. Your judgment will not simply be about the individual on whom a book is written, but your judgment will weigh the life circumstances that shaped his or her criminal disposition. The My Crime series takes the unknown inmate and presents his or her life for public evaluation.

Each book in the My Crime series is written on an inmate, by an inmate. Each book will progress from the Subject's childhood up through the commitment offense that brought about the Subject's current felony incarceration. Each book, therefore, will offer the big picture of the Subject's criminality as dictated to and written by a fellow inmate.

The My Crime series books are intended to fit into the present-day dialog on crime and punishment. As citizens of a democracy, the understanding we each have of right and wrong is the most essential knowledge we use in taking political positions. Ideally, the justice issued by legislators and interpreted by courts is a justice that agrees with most citizens. If citizens agree with the justice being issued by the government, citizens will promote that justice as truth for the times.

As a society, we do not know ourselves enough to have the right answers on justice. The My Crime series grants you the opportunity to sit and listen to the unknown felon and learn, as if you were on the bottom bunk, about your neighbor and what brought him or her to getting locked up.

Encourage others to read the books in the My Crime series by leaving a review.

I welcome you to visit the webpage dedicated to this series to access additional content for this book and other books in the My Crime series. **Additional content includes phone interviews, book drafts, and supplemental offerings:**

WWW.CRIMEBIOS.COM

Finally, I welcome you to read the last page of this book for information about the producer and publisher of the My Crime series, the East Oakland Times, LLC.

In liberty,

Tio MacDonald

Chief Editor

SPINNER'S STORY

ATTEMPTED MURDER • GREAT BODILY
INJURY

1

A HARD BIRTH

This is my fifth term in prison. I am currently beginning my seventh year of a seven-year sentence. I am incarcerated for great bodily injury and attempted murder. I have been to two different prisons. I always seem to wind up back at San Quentin. A prison that has helped change and mold my life.

My name is Jay Jay and I am from Sunnyvale California. I was born in Santa Barbara California to a lovely woman named Althea. I'm now 53 years of age. Since I have aged I have learned reflection is the key. With that in mind, I will recount my formative years to you.

My mom's family were early settlers to the west. They traveled all over the early frontiers of America. I have two brothers and no sisters. I had a younger brother that passed away before he was a year old due to him not wanting to feed by bottle or breast. The doctors never told my family what he had. I don't think they were able to diagnose it at that time. Either the illness was not discovered yet or the proper medical care had not been figured out.

Some look at being born as this wonderful occasion. My birth was one that was difficult and could have ended in tragedy.

My mother Althea Louise (Lou) was having complications with the pregnancy early on. She was spotting blood at around ninety days during her pregnancy with me. My mom decided to go to the hospital. The hospital was called St. Francis in Santa Barbara. She was sent home but the spotting of blood never stopped. Everyone told her something was wrong. My father took her to the emergency room. The hospital initially wanted to reject her because it wasn't an emergency. They argued for a few and my mom won the battle. They admitted my mom and she was placed in a section of the hospital. We didn't have private insurance so getting her own room was out of the question. They gave her a room she shared with an elderly lady.

Trying to help a lady carry a pregnancy to term was still difficult at that time. There were only crude methods in place. My mother was placed in a hospital bed with her legs raised up in stirrups. She was given medication to relax. They placed her with several pillows under her legs. This allowed her pelvis to remain up and to take some of the strain off her uterus because of keeping her legs in the stirrups all day. This way I would hopefully stay in the womb. The medication stabilized her and she remained in this position for three and a half months.

She was taken care of by the nurses there. They were very pleasant to her and would stop by when they were off their rounds to make small talk with my mom, telling her about what was going on in town and in the latest episodes on T.V.

Despite taking the medication and keeping her in this awkward position, my mother kept cramping and spotting blood. This made all the doctors nervous. The staff at the hospital thought that she would lose me during pregnancy.

Eventually, the stabilizing medication lost its effect. It had been the last resort. She felt water between her butt cheeks and knew it was time. She took her legs out of the stirrups and kicked the pillows out from under her and onto the floor. Her water broke and I came into this world.

✖ ✖ ✖

My childhood was difficult from birth. I was born two and a half months premature. The success rate of a child surviving back then being born that premature was around twenty percent. She couldn't hold me the way mothers usually do when they birth a child. It made her angry and she cried. I can only imagine how strange that felt for her. Looking at her little tiny baby and she couldn't touch me.

I was so small and underweight that they had to put me in an incubator. An incubator was where they placed premature children back then. It's still used today, but now they take the baby out for contact with the mother. Placement in the incubator was done to possibly save my life. The incubator looked like a metal tube that hummed and hissed. The machine had artificial air so I could breathe.

The nurse that was on duty, along with my mom, pleaded with the doctor to get me out of the incubator. The nurse had told my mother that I had a better chance of surviving in my mother's arms. The nurse said that in her experience she had seen a lot of babies die in the incubator. The comfort a mother gives to her child is something that medicine cannot offer. The hospital staff had a few meetings about what to do with me. Finally, a week later I was released from the incubator machine to my mother.

I'm not sure if I was a blessing or a curse being born.

My real father wasn't there when I was born. I did not meet him until some time later in my life. My real father was in Lompoc Federal Prison for check fraud. He was of Scottish and Spanish descent. His name is Jessie Elsworth. He was a Marine and served his country in

Korea. My mom said that he wanted me born on Veteran's day. With all the complications with my birth that didn't happen. I think the truth of the matter is that he just fell in love with another woman and any excuse would do to separate from my mom.

I really felt my mom loved my father. But she had two boys and no real provider. What had occurred was my real dad had stolen their checkbook and signed his name on all the checks. It was federal crime back then. He was locked up and sentenced to prison. So she married the son of the man that accused my biological father of check fraud. That really left us without our father.

I have an older brother named Jimmy who is 4 years older than me. Jimmy and I have always been very close. Jimmy has a different dad. His dad was in the Army and served his country. Jimmy ran cross country during most of his school years. Even though I was younger and smaller than him he tried to include me in his life.

At 6 years old I started drinking booze. It was something I saw my parents do. They seemed like different people when they drank. They would be happy and laugh all the time. This encouraged me to drink. Not to mention that my parents gave me little sips to calm down. When my dad would send me in the kitchen to put ice in his glass, I would take little sips of it. If the liquor was straight with no chaser it didn't taste as good. But when he mixed it with soda it was delicious. I started making my own drinks when my dad was gone.

He never seemed to know I was loaded when he would come home. However one day he saw that the bottle he had just bought was half empty. I was the only one home so he presumed it was me. He asked me if I had drunk his liquor. I was loaded and slurred my speech. I got beat by my dad for drinking his booze.

I don't know if he knew after that all the times I had watered down his booze so I could still keep taking little shots of his liquor and get loaded at his expense.

2

HOME LIFE

Despite everything that went wrong in my first couple of years of life I did have a good upbringing. We lived in Santa Clara which was sort of like scenes you'd see on "Mayberry", an old T.V. show that starred Andy Griffith and Ron Howard. It was a small town that had a small police department. It only had three schools. I met lots of friends and we played all the time. I guess one good thing about the town being so small was that the community was close.

There were vacant fields everywhere. We built forts in the orchards nearby. There was plenty of old wood laying around to help create the forts. We even would name a few of them after WWII generals. Ours was called MacArthur.

The most fun we had was having dirt clod fights. There were also fruit fights from the fields. Can you imagine being hit by a piece of rotten fruit? It has a distinct smell of cheap wine and vinegar.

Sometimes during the holidays we would throw firecrackers at each other. This created its own challenge. You had to light it and then throw it without it blowing up in your hands. We weren't trying to hurt each other but just kids having fun. We even used slingshots to shoot firecrackers off at each other.

We were adventurous but good kids. We hopped trains and had no idea of where we were going. Sometimes we got off of them two or three towns over. We would party with hobos because they were known to give us drinks. In other towns we would just hang out with the other town's kids. There were lots of families where we stayed. There were Portuguese, Mexican, Native American, Italian, Irish, and black American families. We all got along despite cultural differences. When we had disagreements and fought our parents made us make up.

The church we went to on a regular basis was nice. I liked Sunday school. I never knew why my mom would take 45 minutes to an hour to put VO5 conditioner in my hair on our way to church. She would comb my hair over and over again. In the end, all she did was just slick it back. Then the old ladies at church would just mess my hair up by ruffling it. This would always happen within the first five minutes of me being at church.

The older ladies got on my nerves but I found the message of a divine power interesting. The elders would ask my brother Jimmy questions like, "What grade are you in now?" Or, "Are you still a straight-A student?" I, however, would try to hide from the elders at the church.

Mrs. Evelyn, in particular, was a pain in my butt. She would look around and say, "Where did Jay Jay go?" Someone would say he's behind you. Then she would turn around and smile. I would start to walk around her again to stay behind her so she couldn't see me. I always did the same thing until my mom would scold me. My mom wasn't the disciplinarian. My dad was. She would yell at us and he would hit us. At first, it wouldn't be major just a quick swat on the butt by my dad.

Elsie Rose White and Edwin White are my grandparents. They were in an accident and hit by a drunk driver. My mother's mom passed away from the accident. Her father survived.

My mother's brother later overdosed on white china heroin. This could have been because we all have a rare strain of lupus. It runs in our family heredity. This is on my mom's side of the family. I really don't know my father's side of the family. All I really know about my father is that he was a Marine. My brother Jimmy told me that my father was a drunk and was really abusive.

The only man I knew as a dad was a Navy Seal named Jim. He was supposed to go to the summer Olympic games in 1972. He would have left Mark Spitz in the dust. He had this weird attraction to water. Whenever we would drive anywhere no matter what time of day or day of the week it was, if he saw water he would pull over and quickly disrobe and take a swim. I don't know how to swim.

During one of our camping trips at the Russian River he fell through a ten-man raft. A rock ripped right through the raft. All the men on the boat were trying to reach in and grab him. The water was too cold and they couldn't keep their hands in the water for too long. Suddenly he just popped up out of nowhere and said, "Damn that water is cold," laughing. He was a hillbilly from Georgia.

I really feel I might have ruined my dad's life. I definitely ruined his shot at stardom. We were driving down the road one day in his company truck and were passing Washington park. He basically broke in the pool by jumping over the fence. As usual, he sees the water and pulls over and says, "I'm going for a swim." My brother jumps over the fence first and then they grab me and hand me over. Then my dad jumps into the pool. He starts to swim laps underwater. I thought that he was drowning. I jumped in the water after him, thinking I would have saved my dad. What happened was he was on his last breath of air, but seeing me flailing in the water he continued to hold his breath to help me. That created an embolism on his lung, basically scarring his lung tissue.

He went to the doctor and the xrays were bad. They told him he had permanent scarring on his lungs. He would function normally but he could no longer participate in competitive sports.

Because of the stunt I pulled the Olympic committee came to discover that spot on one of his lungs. My dad lost his only hope at making it in the profession he truly loved. All the family felt it was my fault. That caused conflict between his side and my mom's side of the family. The spot stopped him from going to the Olympics that year. He beat the hell out of me when he found out.

The situation with my dad caused so much stress for me. Every time he looked at me it was with disdain. I found a small comfort in stealing their cigarette butts. I don't know how everyone else starts smoking or using drugs but this is my story.

3

DRUGS IN THE 1970'S

I started smoking pot and I also smoked cigarettes. I found marijuana because I was stealing cigarette butts from the ashtray in the house. It was the one that had lipstick on it. I took a couple of drags on it and I knew it was different. Another day while stealing butts to smoke I quickly grabbed another one but found out that one also wasn't a cigarette. It was actually a marijuana joint. My brother could smell the weed on me and said, "You know you've been smoking weed." He would warn me and say, "You know you're going to get into trouble."

I really liked weed. Smoking it made me feel alive. I was relaxed and felt a sense of calm that I wasn't used to before. Most of all I didn't get beat from my dad for drinking his booze. He had developed a breath smell test to see if I was drinking. I remember he used to see me and call me over just to smell my breath. With weed I was able to get away with being high. I got past the breath test from my dad. Pot was good because it helped me get past the butt whippings from my dad too.

The first hard drug I used was snorting coke. My brother had just bought a car. It was a 1974 Dodge Challenger. I was in the back seat and we went to the drive-in theater to watch "Up In Smoke" with Cheech Marin and Tommy Chong. It seemed like everyone there was blazing pot. We were smoking pot. I was so high. A friend of my brother's named Brian pulled out some coke. Brian had worked at Pete's smoke shop. It was a store that sold paraphernalia. The products were allegedly sold for tobacco but we used them for drugs. My brother took down a mirror from the visor. The coke was already chopped up in a vial. He had a straw and used it to snort the coke. The coke woke me up. I was jittery and couldn't stand still. It numbed my whole face. I really didn't like it because I couldn't feel my face. It reminded me of going to the dentist. So coke has never been high on my priority list.

By the time I was 10 I had experimented with a lot of different drugs. I sniffed coke, ate mushrooms, took LSD hits, smoked a lot of weed, and drank a lot of booze. I really wasn't addicted to any of the drugs at that time. It was recreational use. I used them to relax and hang out with friends.

I was a pretty respected kid but being the smallest of all the kids I grew up around sort of put me at a disadvantage. I was knee high to everyone. I don't know if it's from being born premature or genetics. Then I had a small growth spurt. It was gradual of course. When I grew an inch it felt like a foot.

We loved to play baseball. One of the games we played regularly was "pickle." We played pickle with all the kids on the block. It was a good game we could play using our baseball equipment. We would put gloves down on the lawn and they would throw the ball back and forth while you would try to steal a base.

The thing we used to do that pissed my mom off the most was steal her jelly jars. We took her Welch's grape jelly jars and used them as drinking glasses. The drinking jars were filled with liquor and we would go to the tree house to drink and smoke pot. My mom would get mad because we never brought the jars back.

My mom had taken me to the doctors because I was so hyper. It was hard for me to get a full night's rest. The doctor prescribed Dexedrine. He said it would help. The drug calmed me down but it also wired people up. I started passing it around to my friends to get high. They all liked it. This drug made me feel alive. It helped me to concentrate and I didn't worry about the things going on around me. My mom noticed that the pills didn't add up and they were disappearing too quickly so she canceled my prescription and stopped giving them to me. She said that she couldn't afford the drug. It was around $10 a refill. This was the cost of a week's worth of food. After I stopped taking the drug I started getting into more trouble. Later I found out that I have ADHD but it was not diagnosed back then. I was in the early parts of junior high school.

My mama was super intelligent. This gene was passed on to my family. My brother was around six feet tall at the beginning of junior high school. My brother was smart and so was I. The crazy part is like most kids I was so smart that I was stupid.

I can remember when I was a real little guy, around three years old. Back then Santa Clara had a small population and the cities were filled with orchards and fields. There were so many fields of walnuts, cherries, strawberries, and other fruit. There weren't any gates locking in any property. The owners didn't seem to care if you picked a few. You never needed to go hungry. This time was in the late 1960's and early 70's.

4

SILICON VALLEY, CA

There was a lot of turmoil in the world. We were involved in the Vietnam war. I saw so many mothers crying when they found out their sons had been killed. There were funerals at least once a month. The Manson family was in full effect and were all over the news. Their trial was on T.V. every day. Patty Hearst and the SLA also made headlines. But there was one story that kept me up at night. The biggest fear I had when I went to sleep was the Zodiac killer.

My dad had bought us a dog for protection. It would bark every time someone walked past our house. The dog would scare some of the neighborhood kids. It was so funny. Sometimes the dog would leave on its own through a hole in the fence. It would speed around in the fields running and playing.

We would take the dog with us on our hunting expeditions. We tried to hunt squirrels and rabbits in the fields. We didn't have any guns and tried to hit them with rocks. Of course that wasn't easy and gave us a good challenge. We only got lucky about one in every hundred tries.

One day we went out to the fields and played follow the leader. I was wearing some red corduroy overalls. I had on white sneakers with a blue and white striped shirt. It's sort of crazy but I can close my eyes and see the day replay all over again. There was a wanderer or transient out on the same trail where we were. Someone yelled out, "It's the Zodiac Killer!" We all screamed and ran like crazy. We were all passing each other and leaving the girls that were with us behind. I was so small and was running as fast as my little legs would take me. By the time I got to the hole in the fence, all of our parents were outside standing in front of their houses. Everyone was afraid and looking scared. The police arrived and questioned the man. It turned out that it was no one but a transient. But we all were so scared.

I remember falling a couple of times while I was running. I think I still have scars on my knee because of it. I could remember running to my mom and just crying and trembling with fear. I didn't care who was watching me or standing in front of the apartment complex. I sat right there on the porch and peed my pants. I started sucking my thumb and trembled. I was traumatized and never really recovered.

I will never forget that day. I was afraid of getting my butt whipped by my dad but this was a different level of fear. This was the first time I really knew what absolute fear was. It wasn't something I was looking for, but it found me.

My parents moved two months later to Sunnyvale. Our new home was four houses down from the Sunnyvale train station. It wasn't an apartment but a duplex house. The neighborhood was really nice. It was as if we moved from "Mayberry" into "Leave It To Beaver" town. All that was there in town was one post office, a Greyhound bus station, and a Grissos Market that sold pig heads.

5

THE ZODIAC KILLER

You know how there is often one situation that changes your life forever? This one is mine: I created problems by messing with a drifter at the train station. It was Pam's birthday. She was my girlfriend Kathy's sister. My brother and me, two friends, Brian and Robin, and Kathy were drinking. Pam called and said their mom was going to pick up Kathy at Round Table Pizza because it was Pam's birthday. So we all walked to the Round Table Pizza and passed through the train station to Town and Country shopping center. While walking back I had a bottle of Black Velvet in my pocket that we had been drinking.

Out of nowhere, and unprovoked, this guy ran up with a machete in his hand and yelled, "I'm going to cut off your balls." Brian pushed him and we walked around to the other side of the train station. When we came around to the other side of the train station all the passengers looked scared. The guy had been harassing them also. We tried a shortcut home by breaking through a hole in a fence.

I gave Brian a drink and we passed the bottle back and forth. We just sat there and watched the dude. I was angry at this machete-wielding person. The same creep assaulted a kid. All the kid was trying to do was buy a newspaper. The guy kept claiming that the newspaper machines that were in front of the station were his. We went back and talked to my brother, since he was the oldest. My brother didn't want no part of it. I remember the fear I felt that day when I was scared of the Zodiac Killer. I would never feel that fear again.

We decided to take the guy out. So we smoked a joint at my house. Brian and I left and went and got his rifle. Brian had a 22 long barrel rifle. It was a single shot bolt action rifle. He used to call it his "Deer Gun." He put his scope on the rifle, pointed it down in the direction where the creep was and said, "I got a good shot." I had changed my mind and thought that we needed to be more sensible about it. So he put the gun away and we went back to my house.

We smoked another joint and then went to the garage. We grabbed a couple of baseball bats and headed back to the train station. We walked through the hole in the fence. My brother trailed behind us. We tried to hide the baseball bats behind our backs as we approached the dude. I taunted the creep with, "Hey, mister, do you want to cut off our balls now?" I told Brian to hit him high and I would hit him low. We beat the guy really good.

6

AGE TWELVE

B eating the transient changed my life. As it turned out we got arrested by the Sunnyvale police. The police ransacked the house looking for us. Bernice and Harold were an older couple and friends of my mom. They knew what had happened and called the cops. They saw us that night covered in blood. We got arrested and my brother told on us. He told them everything.

I finally hit rock bottom at the age of 12. I was a full-blown addict. All that I wanted to do was get high. I was no longer going to school anymore. I just drank all day long. And now I was going to jail. My mom and dad divorced shortly after that incident occurred on the railroad tracks. I think my mom blamed my dad for what happened to me.

My brother went with my dad and my mom was alone. Jimmy never told me why he chose to go with my dad. But I assume it was because my dad had the money and owned his own appliance business.

In court, we were quickly sentenced to four and a half years for assault with a deadly weapon. I began my criminal career.

7

CYA

I was sent to O.H. Close which is a California Youth Authority prison (CYA) in Stockton. I got right into gymnastics and sports. It was a program they offered and I was bored and needed something to do. After all, I was still a kid and only 12 years old.

I ran track well. I competed in the 50-yard dash and the 100-yard dash. I was the fastest in the 200-yard sprint and I also ran the relay. I played flag football, volleyball, and basketball. I still have the championship K.H.S. trophy and Holl Hall Basketball trophy at home. I remember I made the winning shot from the foul line. I used to shoot with the underhand shot, granny style, like Rick Berry.

I received schooling while in CYA. I progressed quickly from the General Education Diploma (GED) program to being placed in an actual high school diploma earning class. I graduated and attended a college program they had. I earned an Associate of Arts (A.A.) degree in sociology. I accomplished all this by the time I was 17 ½.

So I guess I can say that the state raised me.

My girlfriend Kathy stayed in touch with me for about three years. I got letters and pictures from her all the time. It really made me miss her a lot. She was my first love. The sad part was, through my stay in CYA I never got a visit from anybody. I felt so alone during that time of my life. I craved the contact of my family. The people I felt loved me and would be by my side no matter what. That time never came and I hope I don't hold any resentment deep down in my heart.

✖ ✖ ✖

The day finally arrived for me to regain my life and parole from CYA. Surprisingly it was my dad instead of my mom that came and picked me up. Instead of going back to Sunnyvale as I thought, I moved to Bangor, California to live with my dad on a building lot my grandmom and grandpop owned. The place was 27 miles away from town. To go to the movies or any place else I had to hitchhike. We lived in campers and had to use an outhouse to go to the bathroom. I showered by a garden hose. It was rough, to say the least. I had it better in jail. Yet that was the last place I was trying to go back to. My dad went to the bar every night and got drunk. He would bring home any barfly he picked up. The only upside was that it was really quiet out in the hills but when they would have sex it echoed and made me miss my girlfriend.

I ran away and went to go visit Kathy. She lived just a short walk from my mom's house. When she came to the door I kissed her. We just tore our clothes off and had sex. Before the end, I heard a baby cry in the back of the house. I asked her who was that? She said it was her kid. I was shocked and wanted to see the kid. I saw the baby and understood why her letters got sparse.

While walking around town I saw my brother Jimmy. It had been four years since I'd seen him. He still looked the same only he wore a beard now. He was married at the time. We made small talk and went to his house to get a bite to eat. I left and ran around town.

When I saw Jimmy later on that day he was clearly upset. He told me that dad had called and asked if Jimmy had seen me. My brother told him that he had. I told Jimmy to tell dad that I would get back to him soon but I was having fun looking for old friends. My dad was angry and told Jimmy that if I didn't get back to the property I would be in violation of parole which would mean I would go back to prison. That was the last place I wanted to be so I reluctantly went back. I bought a Greyhound ticket and took the lonely journey back to Hicksville.

My motto became, "If I can't beat 'em, join 'em." I enrolled at Butte Junior College and took some psychology classes. I started hanging out on campus. There were more kids my age there. I met some fine looking girls that liked to drink and party and I chose one as my girlfriend.

Later on down the line, I found out that her brother cooked meth. Her brother and I grew to be friends and he quickly taught me the trade. I learned how to manufacture methamphetamines and now I could get high for free.

8

ANGIE

I was now a cook and had a way to make money. I learned not to be scared while cooking it. That was how people blew up or got burned. I did that for a while but the drug was spreading widely and showed no mercy to anyone. People died every day as a result of the drug.

My relationship heated up with one of the girls I was dating. She was my best hope for getting out of the business and having a normal life. I never knew true love and I assumed she was it. So I got married to Angie. She was my angel. She was not a drug user and only drank wine. I was 25 and it was either now or never.

While out walking around one day I got picked up. I was still on CYA parole. I was scared I was going back to prison. I professed my love for Angie. We got married on the phone. The pastor was on one phone and she was on another phone. It was crazy! I had a phone in each ear. The ceremony lasted about five minutes. She had brought a ring earlier. A cop handed me the ring at the end of the phone ceremony. When I went back to court the judge said, "Oh you're married now. Go and consummate your marriage." He suspended my sentence and told me to go home and be a good man.

We tried to settle into a married life but she wanted to control my life. I started drinking heavily and smoking weed to deal with the new stress. It wasn't long but three years after we said our vows, I was back dealing meth. That was due to me not having money and always hearing her mouth about it. I knew that dealing meth was a simple hustle and made good money quickly. I told my wife she no longer had to struggle paycheck to paycheck. Angie loved the new source of income. She bought whatever she wanted and was off my back. I didn't have to hear anything when I came home.

The deeper into the crank scene I went the less we communicated. I stayed away from home for long hours and days. When she did see me she was concerned about my health. She wanted me just to stay home but I didn't want to hear her mouth.

After a while, I thought I was in a bad area of addiction and decided to go to rehab. It was common for me to stay up for weeks at a time. Rehab looked like a beacon of hope. It was covered by her insurance and my job insurance. My boss knew I was drinking at work and agreed for me to go.

The rehab only lasted 16 days. I thought it was going well. Then I saw Angie's friend Pam. She was the only visitor I had while I was there. I looked at her as she walked down the hallway and I smiled. She had a troubled look on her face. I asked her, "What's up Pam?" She did not reply and handed me a large envelope. I was served with divorce papers. I looked out the rehab window into a car and saw Angie. I threw my hands up in the air. She came in and said she really didn't want to divorce me but it was what the counselors told her to do. Everyone kept telling her that I needed to focus on myself. I was like "Okay" and signed the papers.

That wasn't the only bad news I received in rehab. The house my grandpop and grandmom built had burned up in a fire. My grandmom got out but grandpop didn't make it. My grandmom recounted the incident to me. She said she saw him on fire and he fell at the front doorway trying to exit the house. He had saved her life. The neighbors tried to help save the house but the house was devoured before any real help could arrive. My grandpop died at the scene.

I always wonder if I would have been there could things have turned out different. My granddad was gone. I was not allowed to go to the funeral. The counselors said it would be too much in my early stages of rehab. It hurt me so much not to be there. I was trying to get better but at that time I couldn't focus on anything.

Soon I was healing and wondered where I would go. My family didn't want me to come home because they thought I would start back making meth. They told me that the Alcohol, Tobacco, and Firearms (ATF) and the Drug Enforcement Agency (DEA) were all over the hills. There were explosions in the hills at least once a week from meth labs. I don't know what they were doing wrong but it made the areas where we had cooked the drug hot. You could hear helicopters and police on all-terrain vehicles speeding through the hillside all hours of the day. I knew it was a federal crime to cook meth but what was I to do and where would I go? The meth was the only thing keeping money in my pocket. There was just too much going on in my life and in my head at one time. I stayed away from the hills but I didn't know what to do.

Turns out, I leaped out of the pot and into the kettle...a friend introduced me to shooting heroin.

9

DOPE

Heroin sends a warm sensation through the body. I felt invisible on it. Using was good at first but my habit grew and I got worse. The more I used the more I wanted. I would fill the syringe up full and shoot all of it. The bad thing about heroin is you never know what you got or what it's cut with. At least with my home cooked meth I knew what was in it.

Occasionally I would get a batch of really good heroin. Other times I didn't. I went on serious benders. I OD'ed three times on heroin. I got bolder with each shot I took. A couple of people I knew did die on heroin. I knew that was where I was headed. I knew I needed help and went to a detox at the center of town. If I didn't I was sure I would kill myself.

It was an outpatient clinic. You could leave whenever you wanted to. While in detox I ran into an old buddy who was trying to clean himself up. I used to cook meth with him back in the hills. He was tired of the detox and asked me if I wanted to leave. I was almost at breaking the habit. The monkey was seriously on my back. They would give me methadone to take away the cravings. It worked pretty well at first but my body still wanted heroin. I knew I needed to stay clean. The guy I met there wanted to seriously leave. He kept asking me to go with him. I was like what's the use to hit the streets broke. He told me he had some dope and money buried. It was all I needed to hear and we split.

I started selling dope again but this time I stayed away from heroin. I had no control over the drug. At least on speed I could choose when to use it. On heroin I needed to use just to feel normal in the morning. That was one demon I was glad to rid myself of.

10

DATING

I was making progress in life and started back dating. I met this cute Norwegian girl. She worked as a yoga instructor. She was a little tiny thing that only stood 5 feet tall and probably weighed around 108 pounds. She was a true blonde with light blue eyes. Everything about her turned me on. She had a wonderful bubbly personality.

We quickly developed a strong relationship. Moving in with her was the best thing I did. Or so I thought.

One day she found my stash. I was the typical user and would get high and hide dope everywhere. I had speed hidden all over the apartment. Turns out she was a user also. While I was asleep she would raid my stashes and take what she wanted.

I was on a bender one day and had passed out in the bathtub. I was up for about eight days partying. It was nothing for me to go a week without sleep. How my lady could do this to me is beyond me. All I know was she was pissed at me and I can't remember if I had really done something to her or the drugs were warping her mind. Her way of getting back at me was as follows.

She stuck tacks under the bathroom rug while I was passed out in the tub. She also set off Black Flag pest fogger spray canisters. She had them all over the apartment. She even sprayed a can in the tub water I was in. The cute little girl that I loved so much was trying to kill me.

She had towels duct taped to her feet to stop from injuring herself. And she was fogging her way out of the apartment. I woke up because the water had gotten cold. Stepping out of the tub I felt a sharp pain in my foot. I had stepped on a tack. I started coughing at the fumes. I could smell the poison in the house. I saw her standing in the doorway. She yelled, "I tried to warn you!" I ran over and grabbed the can from her hand. I then pushed open a window. I threw the can out the window. I then went and opened all the apartment windows and front door.

I wrapped a towel around my face to stop breathing in the fumes. I held her in my arms as she started to cry. I asked her if she was mentally okay. All she could do was shake her head, "Yes." I then got dressed. I grabbed all the paraphernalia and drugs from the house and took them to my car. I handed her $2000 and left.

I then took all the stuff over to my friend's house. I needed to go get checked out to see what sort of damage was done. I went to the hospital and checked into the E.R. It took a while but I was finally seen by a doctor. They gave me a shot in the butt with antibiotics and said because I was only exposed to the spray for a short time that I would be okay. When I told the E.R. doctor the story of my Norwegian girlfriend poisoning me she laughed. I thought the doctor was going to call the police. I guess she didn't believe me.

I never called the cops. I didn't need them involved. I hate cops. But I took it as a sign that the woman was poison. I never saw her again.

✖ ✖ ✖

After that I had another rough incident with a girlfriend. This new girlfriend started hanging out with some white supremacists. She told me one day that they wanted to buy some speed. They were from my area but really dangerous people. So at first I was a little skeptical about doing business with them. They would set up drug deals for us to pick up, drop off, or collect money. I remember on one occasion I read in the paper a friend of mine was executed. He was accused of skimming the product. They all took a ride. As they pulled alongside a vacant road my friend was taken out of the car. They blindfolded him and made him lay down. Then they reached down and shot him in the head.

I didn't want to get killed. When I learned about the execution murder I began acting as if I was high and tripping on acid. I made incoherent statements and acted as if I was out of it. I was doing all kinds of weird stuff like asking them if they could see all the trails. The next day I continued the farce saying, "How much of that stuff did you give me? I can't remember anything." After that, I left town.

11

SOBER

I became sober for about two years. Life was pretty good. I was 46 years old living in Gilroy. I was getting Social Security Disability Income (S.S.D.I.) It was just enough money to pay my bills and have a few dollars left over each month. I was getting that because I was an alcoholic and addict. I devoted most of my free time to Narcotics Anonymous (N.A.) meetings and recovery. I was running my own step meetings. I was even sponsoring a few people. The meetings were held at an old Gilroy firehouse. It's now Station 55.

One day this chick comes walking in the door like a breath of fresh air. I couldn't take my eyes off of her. Norman, an N.A. member, was telling me, "Not this girl." I just laughed and walked away.

After the meeting I gave her my number and we started talking. She seemed perfectly fine to me. We started getting together outside of meetings to talk and smoke cigarettes. There were many things on which we could relate. Our conversations would go on forever. We went and ate sushi and would also go out for breakfast.

One day I went to her house to pick her up and she was drunk. I asked her what was going on and she carried on about her husband and her family. She was also upset about the move she had to make from her ex's house back to Gilroy. I told her I would help her out. She gave me $400 and I helped her move.

After moving her back to her mom's, I used to ask the other women in the program to pick her up and take her to meetings. I tried to encourage her to stop drinking. I think at the time we had been dating for six months. She was starting to sober up. She told me one day that she needed someone to go to the motel with her because her mom had kicked her out. So I missed my curfew and ended up staying with her at the motel.

Living with her in the motel was cool. It was only her rules I had to put up with, which was have my butt home every night. I moved in with her and gave up on living at the sober house.

Six months into it I decided to have a drink. It was a bottle of tequila. Drinking led me to getting involved with other things.

I met up with some of my old friends and I was back in the drug game again. We motel hopped around town for two years. She called her mom and told on me. Her mother and I had grown close over time. Her mother sent one of her sons over to the motel to try and talk me into getting sober again. Sobriety lasted for all of about a week and then I was back at it. I guess you can say I have an addictive personality. Her brother made a statement to me warning about some shady stuff his sister was involved in. He warned me to leave her alone. That she might get murdered in the motel. I told him not on my watch.

She lied about me one day and called the cops. It was the classic I hit her story to get me arrested. She was just trying to get back at me for slamming drugs. Maybe she thought it was a way for me to get clean again. I was in traffic at the time and was told by a friend about the police waiting there at the motel for me. When I asked my friend what was going on she said I had a $50,000 warrant for my arrest for domestic violence. That made me livid. I never touched the woman.

I got pulled over one day walking down Monterey Highway. A sheriff driving down the street decided to hem me up. He took me in and I was able to bail out with the help of a bail bondsman. I was given a restraining order and told to stay away from her. I paid no attention to the piece of paper. I didn't believe it was a legal and binding stay away order from the court.

I had nowhere to live. She called me wondering what I was doing. I agreed to go over there and visit with her. She gave me her debit card and asked me to go and buy her a bottle of booze. Instead of one bottle I bought her two bottles and three bottles for me. I brought her the vodka she liked and whiskey for me. I also bought two cartons of cigarettes.

We partied like rock stars most of the night. The next thing I know is we were arguing. I go outside to calm down and smoke a cigarette. I had drunk two fifths and was pretty wasted. I was still mad about the crap she was saying. There were a few people outside. They were just doing their business and I paid no attention to them. She came outside and saw me. There was a guy there with his buddies. He saw my little sweetie. He said, "What up girl?" I shouted to him that she was my girl. He told me to mind my own business. It seemed like she egged him on telling me, "Yeah mind your own business!" Before you know it, the guy and I were fighting in the middle of the street. I guess she was trying to jump in and I slapped her. I sort of really lost it after that.

When I woke up I was a mess. And she was a mess also. We somehow got back into the room we were staying in. Her face was all swollen. She wasn't bleeding anywhere but looked bruised and battered. The left side of my face was totally black. I asked her what happened and all she did was run out the door. The manager saw her and told her to have a seat in the break room. I guess by the looks of both of us they figured we had been robbed. They called the cops and the paramedics. I split. My friends picked me up at Walmart. They drove me to another friend's house to sober up. He said I was going to go back to detox but first he took me to the county hospital emergency room for my face. It was really killing me. When I checked into the E.R. I noticed the staff was moving a lot of people out of the way. The next thing I knew officers charged me. I was being arrested by the Sheriff's department.

✖ ✖ ✖

They booked me on domestic violence. I couldn't bail out because the bail bond wouldn't accept me. I was told I was facing three and a half for the domestic violence with no strike prior. I asked what I did and more so who was the domestic victim. I couldn't remember anything. I had been in a blackout. This of course fell on deaf ears. I was told to tell it to the judge.

I was given a public defender. During the preliminary hearing, my charges changed to great bodily injury and attempted murder. This was a drastic change in charges and time. I was now facing seven to life. I was like what the hell happened? I was told she was beaten beyond recognition. That some of the brain damage she received was life-threatening.

She came to the preliminary hearing and testified against me. She told a horrific tale of being assaulted and beaten by me. I was shocked that someone I had grown so close to would compile such a story. Maybe I did do those things to her when I was loaded. I guess only God knows the truth as to what really happened that night.

The lawyer told me that the District Attorney was offering seven years at 85%. The plea bargain had no life sentence so I quickly took the plea bargain. While I was in jail she sent me a letter trying to say sorry.

The county jail I was kept in was rough. Not only did you have to worry about the inmates you had better watch the guards. I was in a single cell so I really didn't have a celly to worry about. There were some really bad officers in the county jail. They would order everyone around and walk about ready to beat up anyone who didn't follow the rules.

One day when I came back from court I asked to speak to mental health. The court and the time they were trying to give me was getting to be too much. I was losing what little bit of my mind that I had left. The nurse that was walking around summoned the guards. Two officers came into my cell and slammed me around. They hand-cuffed me and dragged me to an interview room. When mental health came to interview me I told them that the cops were going to kill me. One officer looked at the mental health lady and asked her what to do. She had seen me before and told the officer that she had never seen me like that. She chose to call her supervisor to see what to do.

I was in the room now by myself. I was scared because I knew what the officers were capable of. They stripped me naked and then put chains on me. I was taken to a room and given a suicide gown and placed on suicide watch. I wasn't going for it. While they were drag-ging me to the padded room they messed my arm up. I kept kicking the door and yelling for a doctor. The officer came to the door looked at me and said my arm didn't look broke. He warned me to shut up or they would kick my ass again. I wouldn't shut up and they ran in there on me again. This time they beat me till I passed out.

I was finally taken to a doctor and my arm wasn't broken. The crazy part is the same officers that assaulted me are now sitting in the San Quentin reception center for killing an inmate that refused to take his meds.

12

THE END

I have been sober now for seven years. I am waiting to be released. I have some medical conditions but other than that I'm ready to go and find a good woman and settle down. I really want to just go on a cruise and relax, play bingo and shuffleboard. You know just live life. I have spent too many years in prison. I have spent too much time chasing drugs. I woke up one day and told myself this prison and drug life isn't me. I am better than this. I now practice Buddhism. I am a laity, which is a precept holder. It gives me guidelines to live by. I have taken vows in Buddhism. Hopefully, it will keep me off drugs. I can't wait to see how this works out.

HOLLER AT YOUR GIRL

ATTEMPTED MURDER

1

GIRLHOOD

My name is Cjay. I am a transgender woman of color, oppressed by the oppressor. I am on my 21st year of incarceration. My sentence fell under the California "Three Strikes" law. I received thirty-eight years to life for assault with a deadly weapon, a sentence longer than an actual murder. All the result of a "date" gone bad.

I was raised in Kern County, California. Kern County was growing at that time. More than anything Kern County was an agricultural area. There were many open fields to play in. We had a large backyard. There was also a swing in the front yard. I would reach such heights on that swing that I felt I would fly. Kern County was a safe but segregated. In whispers or in private we would call it "Klansville."

Despite being born male I was always a female in my mind. As a child I played with girls. I like playing athletic games, like Jax and Hop Scotch, or feminine games like dress-up. I felt the boys noticed me when we played dress up and I felt special. I felt like I deserved to be special for I was showing my truest self. It felt normal to me as I didn't like being a boy. I was never confused, I didn't like being male. I always knew who I was. Having a penis didn't make me male. Boys were rough and rugged. I was soft, sensual, and special.

My dad was a true alpha male. He stood at a full six feet seven inches tall and weighed 275 pounds. He was a heroic provider and very proud, especially of his children, his four boys. He scared me to death.

My mom was a soft-spoken and loving woman. She provided every-thing we needed and wanted. Our clothes were always cleaned and pressed. We had a hearty lunch to take to school every day. She was also an ear when we needed to talk to someone.

✘ ✘ ✘

One day my dad kept insisting that I go outside and play with the other boys. I told him, "Dad, I'm a girl." He dropped his cigar and turned around swiftly. This revelation did not sit well with my father. It was like I said a curse word. I was surprised he didn't kill me. I could see a vein on the side of his neck pulsate with every heartbeat. He looked for help from my mother, hoping she would say something. She stood up and exited the room.

My father and I argued most the night in an aggressive way. He kept telling me I was playing a game. I told him I was serious, that I was a girl. My mother did not intervene like I hoped she would. My brothers tried their best to avoid the conflict. They knew better than to challenge our dad. By the end of it, I simply let him vent. My mother eventually pulled him into the den and brought his favorite drink, Crown Royal on ice. After that night, he started tripping hard.

Life at home became a bit more stressful. I wonder if he thought he failed. He was the head of the Cary family, one of the most influen-tial persons in town. His son could not want to be a girl. The barrage of words trying to change me never ended. Nearly every time I was noticed he would make a comment. He would talk about my mannerisms and my dress. He always referred to me as "son". In fact, he stopped calling me by my first name and strictly called me son. "Son come here." "Son do this...son, son, son." My father brought my brothers into the effort as well. He had me play the same sports my brothers played. I resisted more out of lack of interest.

Home became an awkward place to be. I was told that none of his sons would be gay. My father was stuck on making me a man. I told him I was not gay. I explained that I was a woman. Eventually I stopped talking to my father entirely. My brain was fried and my heart was broken. My mother became my rock even more as she spoke to me and loved me as I was. My mother was both encouraging and nurturing.

✖ ✖ ✖

My dad was a diesel truck driver. He started off small but was frugal and saved his money. My dad's hard work and my mother's business sense led to the company's success. We got to the point of having approximately twenty trucks, numerous trailers, a diesel lot, and shares in Chevron stock. Owning stock wasn't common in the black community at that time.

The business provided many opportunities for Kern County blacks and the community overall. My parents were likely royalty in town. Prominent persons, such as the mayor, would come by for dinner. Eventually, my brothers joined in the business and helped it grow even more.

My parents owned lots of cars. They were usually parked in front of our four-bedroom home.   My father owned an antique Excalibur vehicle. That car was second to none in our area. It truly could only be outclassed by a Rolls Royce. He also had a Mercedes Benz. My mother chose to drive the Mark IV Lincoln Continental. When they drove together they would take the Cadillac El Dorado.

You can imagine some the bull that came with a prosperous life. Many people envied my parents because of the money and possessions. Everyone seemed to look at our family through a microscope, looking for the smallest misstep. Anything seen became town gossip. We became professional actors when we walked the streets.

Regardless of my father or the pressures of being a Cary, at that time my life was going pretty good. I had some really good friends. We mostly played neighborhood games. Many were sexual in nature. I noticed how the boys would want to play a game called, "Hide and Go Get It." In Hide and Go Get It you would hide and the person who was it would try to find you. Once they found you there was some sexy grabbing or wrestling before starting the next round. Another game was "Doctor and Nurse." The nurse always had the job of seducing the doctor. "House" was likely my favorite game. For House, there was a mommy and a daddy. I always played the mommy. In fact, I always played any role that put the boys on top of me. It was great fun and made me feel feminine. We didn't have intercourse but we certainly were grinding with our clothes on.

My brothers were masculine and would want to wrestle one another all the time. They enjoyed imitating what they had seen on television or they would put on eight-ounce boxing gloves and box the other boys in the neighborhood. My brothers never lost. At times, I would laugh as they knocked around the other kids from the neighborhood. My brothers also knew well the pressure from my father to be hypermasculine.

As one should guess, boxing was not for me nor was it the type of physical contact I desired. I wanted to be held, kissed, and caressed. I did not want my lights punched out or to punch out anyone's lights. My game was flirting. I learned that attracting men was something I did well; it was my strong suit.

The struggle with my father never got better. Me being transgender and named after my father became unbearable for him. I was a son and that was how I was supposed to be. All the arguing and attempts to erase my identity culminated in me being sent out of state to be set straight. I was to be sent to Utah for military training, a type of boot camp.

2

SELF TRANS-FORMATION

W hat I found in instead, was myself at an isolated camp filled with lusty boys. I lasted only two weeks before being kicked out for sexual misdeeds. We got caught getting our grind on. My father was livid and told me not to come home. I was 16 and I didn't know what to do.

Near to the military academy was a town with a job corps. Somehow, I got sent there. I vividly remember driving into town. It was a picturesque type of place, quaint. The streets were lined with trees. Blue mailboxes were found on the corners. Couples were out walking and sitting on their porches. I thought it was great.

Job Corps was a program that taught employment skills. Primarily construction skills were taught. We stayed in single-sex dorms with approximately thirty people in each pod. The shower area was open stall showers where you could see it all. Little did my father know, I was in the best place possible.

At job corps, I began to meet other transgender people. I learned the basic "ins and outs" of being a woman. The guys would flirt with me daily. I learned to use what I had in absolute fashion. I was loving it and loving life. I was meeting people from all over the world and I had all sorts of companionships. I tried every nationality under the rainbow at least once. There were Mexicans, Jamaicans, whites, and blacks. You name him and he was on my plate. I was in heaven. Most of the men I dated were good lovers. I really don't have a preference.

Upon my return to California some years later I was different. I was 19 years old and I looked at sexuality different. I knew money could be made by having sex. A couple of people at job corps taught me that. California was slow compared to the lifestyle I now knew. I was bold and sure of myself.

At this point in my life I didn't care what my dad thought. I was living my life and I didn't need anyone's acceptance or approval. I worked for a short while for the County of Kern Bank. I was hired in a microfilm position for accounts receivable. With the money I made and saved from job corps and the bank, I was independent. I had my own place. It was a tiny one bedroom but it was mine. I also had a 1989 Honda Civic.

Nonetheless, I was not interested in the job. I dreaded waking up every morning to sit in a cubicle. I didn't take long to quit. Using my body could get me further and quicker than a 9 to 5 job ever could. I began a self-transformation toward prostituting.

3

MY MURDER THWARTED

With little time, prostitution brings in the quick buck. I was successfully making $1200 most nights. The downside to prostitution is that it is a dangerous game.

Once an average looking "Leave It to Beaver" white guy picked me up. He took me out to the desert. I thought, "This is a strange place for a date," but since he was paying I was game. We pulled off the main road and drove inland. There were no trees, nor vegetation. The night was shivering cold. The sky was pitch black. It was as if the desert was inhabited by evil spirits or ghosts. I didn't think about these things long. My thoughts were interrupted. He gave me three crisp one hundred dollar bills and we climbed into the back seat. The car was blue and had a blue interior with plush seats. It was an old car he told me he recently purchased at an auction. The car used to be a police car so the back doors only opened from the outside. He got out of the car and shut the door, locking me in the back seat. He went to the trunk and took out a gas container. I sat there staring. I had no thoughts. The moon roof on the car was open. He poured the gasoline inside the car and on me. I was scared, frozen in fear, and gagging from inhaled gasoline. The gasoline smell nauseated me. I was confused. The man took lighter fluid from his pocket and squirt the fluid in my face. I was shivering and feeling numb. I pulled on the door lock to no avail. The door would not open. He took a small brown bag from his pocket, unfurling a packaged Bic lighter. I began to panic. I prayed for mercy. I needed a miracle. The man cursed me with the words "Burn bitch" as he wadded newspaper into a cone shape. He squirted the paper with lighter fluid. Now here is the miracle, which explains why I am alive to tell this story: when he flicked the lighter it burst into pieces. My heart slowed. I began to feel my fingers, as if the extreme cold had left. I could see his frustration. He was looking around for the lighter pieces. He mumbled something that I couldn't make out yet he couldn't put the lighter back together. I stared at the man and prayed and then everything went eerily silent. I blacked out.

The next thing I knew I woke up in the desert still locked in the back seat of the car. The man was gone. The sun was starting to rise. I could see animals running around. Every second it seemed to get ten degrees hotter. I was stuck in the desert in the back of a torture and murder machine. I tried to kick the windows out but they were reinforced. I tried climbing back into the front seats but the divider between the front and back seats was now locked. I searched around the car for water and food but found none. All I could do was hope and pray another miracle would come. I sat trapped in that car for three days.

I honestly give thanks to God for my survival. I saw a couple hiking through the area. I waved frantically for them. I was found by God's grace. They called for medical assistance and the search and rescue team came to my aid.

While sitting in the hospital I was questioned by the police about the events but I could not tell them I was prostituting so I turned silent. I gave them vague descriptions of the guy and the events and I was released from their interrogation. I was dehydrated and had not eaten or drunk anything all that time. A nurse provided an I.V. for my fluids. I had burns on my body from the gasoline. For the burns, I was given an antibiotic rub to apply on my skin. The nurse told me I was blessed to not have succumbed to the desert heat. I think it was God that saved me. There is no other explanation. The lighter was new. It should not have shattered. God saved me from a fiery death!

4

THE DOWNWARD SPIRAL

Now prostituting shined a whole new light on me, a dark light. My mind tripped and wouldn't allow me to fully do the job. I was afraid on the hustle. I was afraid of people and what people are capable of doing.

Being raped is common when you work the streets. You will always come across idiots that want to role play. Part of their sick fantasies are rape scenarios. They get turned on by it. I can't tell you on how many countless dates I experienced these violations. Here let it also be known, I consider it rape when you encounter a date that refuses to pay afterward!

At the time, my recreational drug use was what I considered normal. I wasn't addicted. I would smoke weed now and then and, of course, have drinks. Nothing heavy at that time in my life. Things changed when my brother Craig died. He was murdered in 1980. He was 17 years old. Craig is around one year younger than me. Craig was murdered in a drive-by shooting in Kern County. The police never found out who killed Craig or why he was killed. His death gravely impacted the whole family. It was the beginning of the end of my mother and father's 35-year marriage. They constantly fought over why he died. I don't know if my mom blamed my dad or vice versa. The issue was the razor blade that cut each of them to the bone. I tried to stay away. I had too much pain in my head and heart at that time.

As soon as I picked up the pieces from losing Craig, "Bam!" I was slapped again. In 1982, my second brother was killed. Kevin was killed in an Amtrak train accident in Tulare County. He was my rock and his death hit me like a sledgehammer. I could always count on Kevin. When Craig was killed two years earlier Kevin kept me from walking off the edge but now he was gone. I never felt so abandoned and alone in my life.

It was at that time that I went into a shell. I didn't understand anything. I was a walking zombie. The only thing that kept me going was strong mind-altering drugs. I began to use drugs heavily to take the edge off and calm my nerves. Try to understand that drug use in the 1980's was cool. It was like the 1960's hippie days all over again. It was what the cool and hip crowd did. It felt like there were never any overdose drug-related deaths at the time. That was until PCP came on the scene.

I used the drug PCP because it was the most effective. We called it by the street name, "sherm." It was the only drug strong enough to calm my nerves and all the B.S. going on in my head. I loved the drug because of its potency. PCP allowed me to forget the events happening in my life. It filtered all I couldn't filter naturally. It gave me a feeling of an out-of-body experience each time I used it. It provided a sense of strength, a false sense, to battle against the depression filling my heart. Soon it became a part of my every waking day. I was high on sherm all the time. The sudden deaths of my brothers were submerged by the drug. Their deaths took me down a deep and dark spiral.

PCP and prostitution went hand in hand. I was able to perform any task requested by dates. I needed sherm daily to block my conscience from evaluating the tricks I was performing. Sherm would blur faces so I wasn't sure what I was doing or who I was doing. Drugs over money became my main goal. Plus, I felt a comfort giving and serving. It gave me a sense, though a false sense, of being loved.

I did not have any PCP induced "rage trips" as seen in the media. Stories of people biting chunks off their own flesh or running around naked through the streets did not happen with me. I would smoke enough sherm to tranquilize an elephant. Even the good stuff that would leave people in zombie mode had a minor effect on me. People called zombie mode "getting stuck." What happens is a person's body freezes and won't move. I wanted to reach such a stage. I hoped to feel that way. However, I guess I was lucky to not have had such a trip. My highs were peace filled with a sense of joy and exhilaration. I wanted happiness and I believed that using was the key.

Drugs numbed my thought processes and my pain. I knew it wasn't good to use as I was. I did not believe it would be a permanent fix but it was there and I took it on completely. I was in self-destruct mode and had drugs on me 24/7 but not once was I caught.

My mother was also going through serious stages of grief. Her two boys, her wondrous and talented sons, left life before her and she was inconsolable. I listened to my mother and attempted to comfort her. She was grieving the loss of her two deceased sons who had passed within two years of each other: Craig my younger brother and Kevin my older brother, my rock.

Mom wouldn't stop crying. She would say to nobody, "I wish Craig was here to do this for me" or "If Kevin were here, that wouldn't have happened." The chores of life went on all around her but my mother no longer had the support she knew and in the place of the love and support known and felt, was deep grief and overwhelming loss.

I began to feel useless at home. My mother could not hear my words.

She became unresponsive and mentally isolated. I was grieving as well. I also felt misery. Nevertheless, she was a wall, a wall that I could not climb nor push over. I knew my mother loved me and I am certain her intent was not to hurt me. She simply could not see me. I was there to love her but she saw right through me to her grief. Her grief was all she could see for it pooled in the tears of her eyes.

My mother never displayed any difference between the love she held for my brothers and me. From childhood, she had been my best friend; she showed love when my father showed anger and shame. She was always reassuring; she would say that everything would be okay. Now her reassurance and comfort were gone. Although she never said it, all I could think was that she needed a man's hand. She needed the comfort of a man and I, as a woman, was invisible to her.

Most transgender women I met did not know the feeling of being out in their femininity and being loved by family. More than often families tried to change us or threatened us to change. Please remember I am not talking about today's world of the openly transgender teen or child. I am talking about a time when transgender people and homosexuals were thought of as works of hell or mentally ill.

My brothers accepted me unconditionally. We used to talk about my gender. My brothers encouraged me to be who I was. They said that dad, in time, would understand. They helped me to feel loved and accepted. My mother did too. With their deaths, I lost all three.

5

L.A. LIFESTYLE

I needed a venue change so I got in my car and drove to Los Angeles. LA wasn't totally new to me as my father and I traveled through much of Southern Cali searching out different enterprises. I also had family in L.A. to help me get on my feet.

Looking for work in L.A. proved futile. I wasn't interested in most the available jobs so I had no money. Eventually, my unemployed status didn't sit well with my extended relatives. In fact, my younger cousins would cite me as an example of why they should get to loaf around. I knew I had to go.

The LA streets were much different and more dangerous than Kern County. From gang-bangers looking for a quick buck to psychopaths, it was important to know the ins and outs of the L.A. streets in order to avoid becoming a homicide. I took my time.

Women of all ages sell their bodies in Los Angeles. I met women in their 50's who said they had been ho'ing since age 16. Some of them took me under their wings and showed me how to operate. I learned where to go and where not to go. I learned the best places to take a date.

Not every woman is happy to see a transgender gal pop up on the scene. Of course, with all of us working it was also a matter of economics and I could certainly hold my own and then some on the prostitution hustle. I made money they could match but none tried to challenge me physically. They knew I would wreck their world.

Propositions for kinky acts increased ten-fold in L.A. Often the requests would blow my mind. Golden showers, fecal squats, S&M you name it. All these "johns" were ready to pay, but on some cases I drew the line; most I didn't. Being an awake and conscious hooker is not an easy job. You have to numb an inner voice to do it.

I started to build a client base. I got my grind on to the urban beat of West Hollywood and to the decadent disco of Beverly Hills. When things got slow I would send myself to Figueroa, the most well-known ho stroll in L.A.

Figueroa was a dangerous stroll that brought fast money. Sometimes the cash would come in so fast my head spun. Sometimes I found myself wanting to prostitute for the feeling it gave me. Other times, as earlier stated, I found myself weighing the money offered against a john's perverse request.

I was working seven nights a week and bringing in thousands of dollars, often in a single night. I spent my money as fast as it came in. I enjoyed luxurious sheets so I rarely got a motel. Hotels all the way. I enjoyed both the Hyatt Regency and the Waldorf Astoria. I always ate out for there was rarely time or mind to cook. You have to buy new outfits to wear also. I always bought top of the line clothes and heels. I needed the best make-up and lingerie. Plus, I needed to buy wigs. One will never understand how expensive wigs are until they become a frequent new purchase. Finally, I had to buy drugs and as my money went up so did my habit. I could spend great sums a day on getting high.

Another predominant character on the streets of L.A. was the pimp and every pimp wanted me in his "stable." A stable is the line of women a pimp has working. The pimp is supposed to protect and provide for his women. The flip side to the good is a dramatic bad, for pimps expect all money made from walking the streets to go to them. Therefore, it was protection at a price, a very high price. I didn't need protection as I could take care of my own business.

The pimps came after me like flies to doo-doo. In their close observations, they saw the money I was making and wanted it. I stayed independent. I was entreated by all, threatened by some, and nearly killed by another. The pimp who nearly killed me ambushed me with his goons. His goons never left his side so I could not win. On a later encounter, he pistol-whipped me. He hit me repeatedly across the face and in the stomach with his gun. I was kidnapped and kept in a garage for nearly a week. Every day he would talk to me about how he cared for me and all his women. He said he wanted me safe and he wanted to protect me. I had to work under him but as soon as my chance came I left. That happened during a prostitution sting. I left Figueroa with nothing but the clothes on my back. I couldn't imagine selling my ass and then giving the proceeds to an animal.

I left Figueroa and moved up towards La Sierra, another hoe stroll. La Sierra was nothing like "the Fig" so I supplemented my income by stealing the belongings of dates. Some would pass out after sex. I would pack all their belongings in a pillowcase and leave them butt naked in the room. This was low of me but I knew they wouldn't call the police. In a short time, I recovered myself from the brutal losses of Figueroa. I knew how to get money.

Not too much time later I moved to an apartment in West Hollywood to live with other ladies who were also working the streets. There were five of us and we had an immaculate spot that cost a pretty penny but I was making more than enough. The single rule for the house was that no dates be brought there. We used the streets for dates and we vowed to keep our home safe.

The dates at that time in West Hollywood were brutal. The men were becoming evil and cheap. Some of the women couldn't keep up. Eventually, these women became a burden to my finances so I removed myself from communal living and freelanced at work and at finding places to stay.

By this time, I had become a veteran of the hoe hustle, the drug game, and the way of criminal enterprising. I found a comfort zone. People trusted me and confided in me. I was accepted by all the "throw-aways" of this world.

I began to do something I hadn't done for some time: think! My parents raised me right and though we had our differences they loved me. I claim full responsibility for my own decisions and mistakes. I was acting a fool on my own accord. I was living contrary to how I was raised. I was doing what was contrary to my parent's wishes. I was in a daze. I thought solely in the present and in what I was experiencing at the moment. I hurt from my brothers' deaths and I struck out on my own. Now the care I knew growing up was shaping me into being a comfort for those truly at rock bottom, although I was at rock bottom with them.

By that time, I had been raped too many times to count. I never reported a single one. Mostly I just wanted to be paid but men often took me for their personal punching bag. I got used to it. Men would beat the hell out of me. I was used sexually in ways beyond speech almost every day. I was passed around and kicked out the door like garbage. Waking up to this took me time and age.

Drugs were still the major focus of my life. My drug focus did not change at the time; however, my drug of choice did. Sherm was a drug I would still use. Sometimes, I would use it to the point of no return, waking up unaware of my location, who I was with, or what I had been doing. Those times I often found myself robbed. Crack cocaine, "rock," was my new drug of choice. The more I used the more I needed. 100 plus dollars a day of crack rock found itself in my pipe.

I knew I had a monkey on my back. The drug game and working the streets became too much but also opened ways for me to meet new people, people who were looking to clean up their lives. Meeting such people offered a seed of hope for how I could be. Most people I met were ex-prostitutes. Most had the same experiences I had, of being used and abused by all around them. I was tired but I saw that transformation was possible.

For me, most of my criminal activities were based on the need to get high. Most of the work I did was under the influence of drugs. Drugs were the Dr. Jekyll and Mr. Hyde of my life. Drugs settled down my nerves and made me feel at ease. Drugs provided comfort and even stability. However, as I needed drugs the drugs seem to need me so I had to get them and getting them brought me to the streets and to crime.

6

CALIFORNIA PRISONS

My prison career began with a four-year sentence. In 1987, I began serving time at California Men's Colony East (CMC) for burglary. I got caught with a man I thought loved me. He wanted a quick score because his money was low. We climbed in a house through a window and came out the front door with pillow cases of loot. Someone must have seen us for the front door is where we met the police. I was given a two-year sentence for which I served fourteen months.

I paroled in 1989. I started violating my parole right away. There weren't any new charges I simply kept violating parole. In the 1980's and 1990's prison was a place for transgender women of color to stay and be safe. We all stayed at designated prisons and we got along well. We learned to help one another. I was blessed to learn the true meaning of transgender sisterhood in prison.

Most of my time was served at California Men's Colony (CMC) and Vacaville. These two prison populations welcomed us. They were safe places to sleep at night. There wasn't much concern about rape so they offered a safe place to recover from whatever you were going through. We could get healthy from our time on the streets.

Employment for transgender women wasn't easy to get at that time. We were not treated with human regard. Most of us prostituted. We would take money or drugs from johns in return for sex. We put ourselves at risk of harm and incarceration. Usually, I was ready to go each time I was sent back to prison.

It is a sad but true fact that most of my medical attention was received at California corrections facilities. I had no medical insurance so in prison, I would receive the health benefits most people received with employment.

Prison also was a great opportunity to meet new people and catch up with old friends.

In the 1990's, conditions inside prison began to change. New sentencing guidelines and mandatory minimums brought about a rapid sentencing. Personnel transitions of guards and medical staff added to a changing climate in which transgender women became targets.

Guards often would let violators approach us or enter our cells. These encounters were ruthless. Violators often times would come up the losers, especially if they hadn't brought their goons to strike us down when we proved victorious. Violators would think twice about fighting me. I had been through a lot of dirt, plus I was born male. If a man lost a fight to a transgender woman, he never lived it down. His reputation was broken. Therefore, most men would only fight a transgender woman with a support-team in tow.

✖ ✖ ✖

One thing that never changed no matter what prison I was in was the men's need for sex. The men are horny and need sex. I chose to give it to them. I could have made good money if I wanted to but what I wanted was a feeling of love. I honestly did experience real love in a couple of relationships. Other relationships were for convenience or protection.

Some men in prison are the most low-down, wickedest people imaginable. For a period, I was being raped by a man and his crew. They raped me all night. Every one of them took his turn on me. I couldn't say a word to the prison guards for snitching is against the prison code. I became a victim and each night I was raped.

A sweet man in a nearby cell saw my predicament and faced the leader. He claimed me as his own. I am not sure how things were straightened out or if they had beef before I became involved, but he saved me.

I found true love with this gentleman. He helped clean me up and he made me his lady. After six months time, I realized that I loved him. He was the angel that rescued my wounded soul. We stayed as one for a time until I paroled.

From that point on I sought out good men, not abusers. I learned the difference between men's lust and men's love. Men in prison will lay up with you and make love all night. The sex can be magical and brutal at the same time. The next day, he will be up early and out at the visiting room talking with his wife and children. Men will do this in a blink of an eye. After getting roused up with his wife, he'll cut the visit short and be at your ass trying to get more. Most of the time I complied. Nowadays and for some time if a man has a wife and kids he is off limits for me. I am not a home-wrecker.

7

MY CRIME

Today I have been in prison for over twenty-two years. I am in prison for assault with a deadly weapon and because of the three-strikes law I have a sentence longer than a first-degree murderer. I will tell what happened.

I was in Kern County, Bakersfield. The day started off as usual with me on my hustle. It was daytime and slow and I was looking forward to evening. The freaks coming out at night is definitely true in the prostitution racket. There was a man sitting on a bench on our prostitution stroll so I knew he was looking for a date. I walked up and down the stroll shaking my ass but he simply sat there. I did not believe him to be a cop because there were no cars around for back up. I asked him for a light and I began to flirt with him. He was distracted from my words and gave the appearance of looking for someone. At that time I was using methamphetamines and my addiction was really gnawing at me. I needed to get high so I got a bit more aggressive with the guy. I figured he would like it once he tired. However, the conversation stayed aggressive and turned belligerent. He began to insult me and curse me out. I turned away and walked to my truck, holding an internal dialog as to my next move. The guy upset me so I decided to rob him. I grabbed my "Get Right" stick, a lead pipe, from my truck and moved on him for a jacking of his possessions. "Give me your wallet," I yelled. My goal was a quick come up without doing anything to him. As soon as I saw the whites of his eyes he took off running. I was wearing my full ensemble of high heels, dress, and wig so chasing him too long was not possible. I threw the pipe at him and, to my amazement, the pipe struck him on the side of the head. The man hit the ground fast allowing me to catch up to him. As he lay there bleeding, I rifled through his pockets. He had a wad of cash in his hand. I was scared to take it from him as he lay there helpless and bleeding. The incident happened swiftly. My heart was beating one thousand beats a second. My head was overloaded with thoughts. I actually robbed someone and hurt him without ever having that intention. I left the money in his hand and instead grabbed the pipe, not wanting to leave evidence. I ran back to my truck, a 1989 Dodge purchased by a date for me from the Dodge showroom floor in Bakersfield.

I started the truck and tried to drive calmly away. I took a few deep breaths as I drove to try and slow my heartbeat. It was a trick I used after taking a big hit of speed or crack. As I sat at a red light waiting for it to turn green my front windshield exploded. I was shocked into maximum alert. Then my driver side window exploded. Glass flew everywhere like raindrops. Next, I saw a ball of fire pass by my face. There were no other cars around, there was nobody visible until my ears alerted me from where the shots were being fired. Crouched beside a building was a Kern County police officer. He ran into the middle of the street and continued to shoot. My fight or flight impulse kicked in and I floored the truck's gas pedal.

In no time at all, I had three police cars behind me and a helicopter above me. I knew I would not get away but I also did not want to be shot. I began looking for a safe place to pull over. There was an intersection with a 7-Eleven. Students from California State University Bakersfield were all over the area, celebrating. I tried to make a sharp turn into the intersection but lost control. The steering wheel had a mind of its own and the brakes seemed to give out. The truck flipped over an eight-foot-high fence and dove head first down a river embankment. The truck ended up face down with the tail in the air. I could see water rushing nearby. I slid out the driver side door and ran toward a fence that enclosed the river. Running through the river seemed to be my only exit. The helicopter could be heard overhead and now I heard the sound of barking police dogs. I figured the man must have said I had a gun or that I had tried to kill him. I ran for the water. Officers stood watching on the other side of the gate. The water current was very strong. I removed the wig that I loved and cost me sixty-five dollars. Why I was thinking about a wig is beyond me. The dogs also watched me as they stood on the river's edge.

I exited the other side of the river. The journey was long and upon my arrival police cars pulled up with sirens and lights blazing. They screeched to a stop and rushed at me with guns drawn. In little time, I was on the ground with a knee in my back and punches and kicks decorating my body. I wasn't moving. I was in shock. They had the audacity to call me nigger. I really think if people weren't there it would have been worse. "We caught you black assed faggot," are the words by which I was lead to the squad car.

The police station brought on equally abusive treatment. I was handcuffed to the floor and abused.

To the man I harmed, I am eternally remorseful. He was a husband, father, son, and brother. I didn't know him, nor he me. My twisted way of thinking brought significant harm to his person and his relationships. For all of that I am truly sorry.

✘ ✘ ✘

One thing O.J.'s case taught most Americans is that freedom is possible if you have money. I had no money so I was issued a public defender from the state. For the preliminary hearing I entered a not guilty plea. Trial was set to begin in two-weeks. While in the holding tank, my preliminary public defender came to speak with me. He had barely touched my file as the papers he brought to review with me were unruffled and pristine.

His face was aghast as he read the police report. He told me, "Look we do not have a chance in hell to win this case. I suggest a plea bargain." I knew I was guilty of the crime so I was willing to plea to a lesser crime. Neither the judge nor the D.A. would hear that.

The trial started that day. I arrived in court at 8 a.m. We quickly picked the jury. The trial was over before lunch. The victim testified. The officers described my flight which brought about an accident causing the state damages. There were no more witnesses and both sides closed their case. The jury deliberated for a total of thirty minutes. I was found guilty beyond a reasonable doubt.

At my Romero hearings, an evaluation of my prior strikes, the judge declared that I was exactly the type of person for whom the Three-Strikes law applied. He felt I was remorseless and my explanations of the crime did not make sense. I was sentenced to thirty-eight years to life, twenty-five years for my third strike and thirteen years for enhancements.

When I reflect on the night of my crime I feel blessed to be alive. I truly believe if we had been in a location without other people, the police would have killed me.

8

SISTER TALK

P rison isn't designed to build you up, it is designed to tear you down. An inmate needs to believe in herself and learn to rebuild. Building yourself is the only way to make the time rehabilitative.

Here are the prisons in California where I have spent a large part of my life: I have been to Vacaville, a medical facility; I have served time at R.J. Donovan, located in San Diego; I have gone to Jamestown, which is better known as a fire camp; I was at the oldest California prison, Folsom State Prison; I was housed at Lancaster (California State Prison) when it was black operated (most prisons are staffed by whites or Hispanics); I also stayed at the deadly level 4 prison in Tehachapi; today I am housed at San Quentin.

Through the Restorative Justice curriculum offered at San Quentin I now more fully understand the harm brought about by my ways. I understand and feel a responsibility to the victim, his family, and the community I lived in. I have shame and embarrassment for what I did and I will make amends in whatever way I can.

I have missed out on much of life, life's simple treasures. I missed the family gatherings, graduations, marriages, births, and sadly, funerals. I missed the funeral of my niece who passed young. I missed the funerals of both my parents and my grandmother. Each of these three persons raised me, suffered for me and beside me. I will always love and miss them. Being absent from them in their final days is something I have a hard time forgiving. Guilt will forever be a lamented but integral part of my soul. I do not believe it will leave me for they deserved better. I should have been there to ensure they were laid to rest with dignity. They loved me in life, I simply hope they can forgive me in death. I was truly out of control.

I have twenty-two years in prison and I'm fifty-eight years old. My body feels the aches and pains. I never thought getting older could be this difficult. Freedom, however, isn't all about physical movement. Personal growth can make one free. Living in God's grace can make one free. I have wanted to be a better person and that began with me forgiving myself and facing my own personal demons. I am a transgender woman of color. I am not a criminal. As I look back over my years of life I consider my need to feel accepted. I sought acceptance or value through drugs, through crime, and through sex. I no longer need anything exterior than God's love. God's love sustains me.

I live recovery every day. The things or stimulus I thought to be important in my younger years now have little meaning for me. Prison has more downs than ups but although I am in prison, I feel free. I have a sense of purpose in life. I have faced the sexual abuse, physical abuse, and drug abuse I knew in times past. I have learned to accept myself and forgive myself for my mistakes. I have also learned to forgive those that harmed me and to seek forgiveness from those I have harmed. I am deserving of real love. God loves me, this I know, as much as He loves anyone else on this planet. I am worth it.

I am serving thirty-eight years to life sentence. Without the three strikes law, my case would have carried a seven-year maximum. My sentence will not destroy me! I think about the harm I did and did not get caught for and I weigh it all on a cosmic scale of justice. I feel no bitterness. The pains of age and the pain of being told day in and day out what to do aren't becoming easier but looking myself in the mirror has become a gift to me from on high.

Today I want all my sisters to know that you are beautiful and unique. You are one of a kind, created from God's grace and love. God makes no mistakes. Be good to yourself. Through pain and fire get yourself together now!   Tune into your spirit and get your hands dirty, rid yourself of junk. Shake out any mental handicaps a lover, boyfriend, or whoever has put on you. Accepting yourself will change your thinking. Go to self-help groups! Align yourself with what is offered by the community. Get yourself together and then you will find new possibilities. You will find someone that is going to love you the way you need to be loved. You got to do the work in order to receive the love and life you deserve. Love yourself! Love life! And remember to "Holler at your girl!"

HOOD TO HEELS

GANG RELATED MURDER

I

LAWRENCE

FIRST MEMORIES

My name is Lawrence Fuller. I was born in Shreveport, Louisiana. I was, however, raised in Los Angeles, California for most of my life. I confess that I don't remember much about my earlier years in Louisiana, but I do recall being on a train bound for Cali with my mother and older brother.

My mother and father divorced when I was a baby, so I have no memories of us as a united family. There were no picturesque moments of us gathered around the Christmas tree singing carols and opening Christmas presents. Nor were there memories of us all sitting around the dinner table laughing, joking, and sharing with each other how our day went. In other words, there were no postcard, picture perfect family moments.

In fact, aside from the train ride, my earliest memory was entering the project housing complex known as "The Pueblos." It was also called "The Bottoms." Believe me when I say it lived up to the moniker.

Upon my arrival at the Pueblos, the first thing I saw was two of my uncles at the top of a flight of stairs fighting and attempting to throw each other down those stairs. My mother told them both to stop fighting and say hello. "Hi," they said, and then immediately recommenced fighting. Little did I know, that such behavior would become commonplace in my life.

The dirty, trash-strewn projects infested with drugs, gangs, and graffiti, were my corner of America. We lived with my grandmother, Queenie, and my two uncles in a two bedroom apartment. Still, at the house, there always was a fluctuation in the amount of people staying with us, but the total number of people generally ranged from eight to ten.

Like almost every other family living in the projects, our family received welfare and food stamps. For additional money, my mom always had a job or relied on a boyfriend who may be a drug dealer or a gang banger. Because of my mother's hustle and resourcefulness, her children always had nice clothes or the latest toys.

When I was three, my mother was involved with a "Blood" gang member and became pregnant with my little sister. The weirdest thing is, my older brother, younger sister, and I, all have birthdays in August. In fact, my older brother and I share the same day, August 30th. My sister was scheduled to share the day as well but was born early on August 4th. Each of us is three years apart.

I recall one time almost burning down my room. I was bored with nothing to do, so I started playing with a lighter. Suddenly, the curtains caught on fire. My mother and grandma were visiting one of my uncles who was locked up in Lancaster prison. I received the worst ass whipping I've ever had in my life. My mom beat me with a snake skinned belt. That incident almost caused CPS to take my brother, sister, and me from my mother and grandmother. I will never forget it.

2

QUEENIE

At that time, I didn't realize that my grandmother was a straight gangsta. She sold drugs and always had the neighborhood crackheads bringing her the latest stolen stuff. Everybody in the Pueblos knew my grandmother. Her name was Queenie and her name carried a lot of weight.

I was young at the time, so I didn't know much about what was going on around me. I knew that Queenie loved to drink and party. I thought she was an alcoholic. Queenie would party on most nights with her drunk friends and bark orders to people and they would rush to do her bidding. When she was drunk, she was cool and fun, but when she was sober, she was mean and straight to business.

The first time I ever saw her make crack from cocaine, I thought she was just boiling milk for my baby sister. I later learned that you don't make milk with baking soda. One of my aunts was sprung off crack and always found her way to our place when my grandmother was cooking it up. I believe my aunt was Queenie's tester.

I never actually saw Queenie give crack to anyone, but there was always a lot of traffic in and out of our place. Sometimes, I would even see Queenie on the other side of the Pueblos where the gang-bangers hung out. The Pueblos was Blood gang territory. To this day, I don't know if she was a Blood or if they just had respect for her. Or, maybe it was because they knew that she was the mother of my two crazy uncles. During that time, my uncles constantly were in and out of jail for either drug sales or gang-related activities.

I've seen Queenie be ruthless and hit people or send people to beat up those who ended up on her bad side yet she was also kind-hearted. She would give to those who had nothing. I know she fed plenty of families in the Pueblos. That is one of the reasons why she was so well loved.

This may not be a big deal for some, but I remember when I was five years old and met my biological father for the first time. As an aside, age five is also when my stepfather came into my life. My biological dad had driven up from Texas and was worried about his rental car. Queenie told him not to worry. She called two drunks over and instructed my dad to buy them a case of beer. She told the drunks to watch the car overnight. When we came out the next morning, they were sitting by the car protecting it. As Queenie approached, they greeted her like royalty. They wanted her to know they'd done what she had said.

3

FINANCIAL STRUGGLES

I was eight years old when we moved from the Pueblos. My mother and stepfather decided to build a house. The ironic thing is, the area we moved to was no better than the projects. Yes, we had a home instead of an apartment and everything inside was looking nice, but the surrounding area had the same problems. Graffiti was posted everywhere. The alleys were infested with trash and dirty syringes. Drug deals were conducted openly for everyone to see. Robberies were committed and crackhead prostitutes sold their bodies on the streets for the next fix. There is no doubt that the neighborhoods I lived in had a profound influence in abetting my entry into criminal enterprising.

For a time after we left the Pueblos, we no longer received welfare. During this period, my mom tried to open her own business. It was a candy store. Things went well and I didn't feel like the poorest kid in the world. The bills were getting paid and we had food on the table.

Sadly our new found prosperity turned an about-face when my mother became sick with kidney disease that ultimately resulted in kidney failure. It's crazy how one moment you can be up, then, the next moment, you're at the worst point of your life. Managing the store put a strain on her and as a result, the store began to fail and eventually flopped.

My stepdad worked in real estate. He struggled to care for my mom, work, and handle all the other responsibilities that arose. He loved my mother and would cater to her. He provided her with everything she wanted. Still, his job performance suffered and he wasn't bringing in as much money. By the time he would sell a house, all the money he earned was consumed by the steadily mounting bills. In the end, we would be as broke as ever.

My mother had to go back to the county for assistance. We were back on welfare. Four kids were living in the home now. By now, my mother had given birth to my youngest brother, yet the welfare office only gave my mom food stamps for my sister. My mom unendingly complained that there was never enough. At the time, I was extremely embarrassed about us having to use food stamps. My mom would say, "Your ass might be embarrassed about these food stamps but they're feeding your ass."

There were times when I would have to wear the same clothes over and over again. I even wore my brother's old clothing to school. There were days I would ask for lunch money and there was none to give. At school, I wasn't able to go on class trips because my family couldn't afford the fee. I remember even thinking, as a little kid, of ways to come up with cash.

The amazing thing is, even when we didn't have money, my mom and stepdad found ways to put food on the table. My brother and I always speculated that they were doing something illegal. We could never prove it but our imaginations would run wild.

4

LIVING WITH DAD

I was ten years old the first time I went to live with my dad. He lived in Dallas, Texas. Living with him was a completely different experience than what I was used to having. While my mother was lenient and allowed me to do almost anything I wanted, my father was a very strict man. He wasn't a street person and he stressed education. He lived in a nice house and had a good life. I lived with him three different times during my adolescence. Although I only lived with him for a few years in total, he had a massive impact on who I am. He would ride my ass about any and everything. There was no half stepping with him. He checked my homework and went to all my parent-teacher conferences to make sure I kept my grades up and was not acting out in school. Each time I lived with my father, I would miss how my mom would just take my word for everything and let me have my way.

5

QUEENIE'S PASSING

One of the most devastating events occurred around this time: my grandmother passed away. When she passed away, she was indeed missed. A block party was thrown in her memory. Things immediately began to change. Queenie's passing was the first death of someone close to me. Part of me felt confused because as a whole, I didn't understand death. Mostly, I felt empty because my grandma, that gangsta woman I looked up to, was gone. Without a doubt, Queenie was the glue that held the family together. She was the backbone. Once she was no longer here, our family fell apart. We all went our separate ways.

6

BEING BROKE

For as long as I can remember, there has been one thing that I have hated more than anything else and that is being broke. As a child, I couldn't stand that I had to walk around in old clothes and old shoes and had no money in my pockets. What made things worse was that all my friends seemed to continually have nice clothes and pockets filled with cash.

One occurrence that affected me negatively was going out with my homies and not having money for food or whatever we were doing. Of course, this produced in me a burning desire to have things. There is no question that my mind dwelt on ways I could come up financially.

Before I turned to crime, I actually tried to do something positive. I was eleven and my big brother was fourteen. We decided to start a lawn mowing service. We were excited and held high hopes of making some good money. We walked about pushing a mower asking people to allow us to mow their lawns. I guess seeing two black, dusty looking kids wasn't a welcoming sight. Even still, the resistance we felt didn't deter us. We hustled for two months before giving up.

At this point, I made a conscious decision to change my circumstances. I was done with having nothing. I was done walking around looking busted and broke. I knew the only way for me to really come up was to step my game up. That's precisely what I did.

7

ELEMENTARY SCHOOL DROP OUT

I 've hated school since elementary. There was a mixture of two things that influenced my outlook on school. First, I remember fifth-grade graduation. Throughout the ceremony, I scanned the crowd excitedly, hoping to see at least one person from my family. I couldn't find anyone. Needless to say, disappointment consumed my heart. With about five minutes left before the ceremony ended, my mother and stepdad frantically rushed through the doors. My mother carried a camera in her hand and was pushing people out of her way. When she got to the front of the crowd, she shouted, "That's my baby up there." She pointed the camera to take a picture of me and nothing happened. After staring at her for a minute, I read her lips say, "Oops." She had forgotten the film. That broke my spirit.

The very next day, my big brother graduated from the eighth grade. My family was on time and sitting in the audience, camera in hand with plenty of film. They were all smiling and filled with pride. I felt that since going to school didn't seem relevant to them, why should it be important to me? Why waste my time when I could be doing other things?

The second and, probably the most important reason, was peer pressure. My friends were always skipping school. Since I didn't want to be looked down on by them, or seem lame, I started skipping school too. It got to the point that I rarely went at all. When I did bother to go, I would leave to find something more exciting to do. Most times, it would end up being some sort of crime.

8

BLACK AND BROWN RACISM

Twelve is also the age when I experienced racism for the first time. My mom decided that our neighborhood was a dangerous place, so she made me attend school outside of my hood. Man, was she wrong. She sent me to East LA. It was the same environment as my own neighborhood. It was infested with the same type of poverty, drugs, prostitution, and gang affiliations; however, it was predominantly Hispanic. I can say, up to this day, I have never heard so many racist things said to me. I was also robbed and stripped of my Emmitt Smith football jersey. The anger, pain, and humiliation I felt caused me to become just as vicious as the guy who robbed me. I started bringing guns to school.

At one point I came face to face with the guy who had taken my jersey. I became even more enraged because he had the nerve to actually be wearing it. He winked at me as if I were a joke. I took off running to where I had stashed my gun. By the time I made it back, of course, he was nowhere to be seen. In retrospect, I'm grateful that he'd left. I know I wouldn't have hesitated to shoot him and would have probably killed him, all over a stupid jersey. Even still, I was robbed because I'm black and I was in a Mexican neighborhood. The robbery and the name-calling happened because of the color of my skin.

The fights and taunts wouldn't stop, so I learned to grow a thick skin. My pride wouldn't let me complain to my parents, so I took my lumps and bruises. Trust and believe me when I say that I gave more lumps than I received.

9

WEED ADDICTION

Age twelve is also when I first used any drugs. It was weed. My mom's candy store was still up and running. A guy named Peanut, who would become one of my closest friends, came into the store to play video games. He wore the strong odor of weed on him. He was fourteen. The entire time he played the game, my brother and I stood behind the counter thinking of a way to approach the subject of buying some weed from him. We were making smoking signals with our fingers at each other.

As Peanut left the store, we followed and asked if he knew where we could buy some. See, we knew about weed, we just didn't know how to go about getting any. Peanut told us not to worry and that he'd be back the next morning.

The next day, we waited and true to his word, Peanut showed up to play video games. Before he left, he gave us a joint. My brother and I raced off and smoked the joint. It was gone in a flash. My brother and I joked and laughed harder than we'd ever done in our lives. Everything was funny. Both my mom and stepdad looked at us with their eyebrows raised. When the munchies hit me, I was hooked.

The next day, we asked Peanut for more. Over weed, a friendship budded. We started smoking every day. It got to the point that we had to smoke before we could do anything. For example, if we wanted to go to the mall, we would smoke before we left. Then, we'd smoke while waiting for the bus. We'd smoke again while at the mall, and once more when we got back to our house.

I never thought it was a big deal because we were not hurting anyone. Then, I started stealing money from family and friends just to smoke. I even began to steal cans and bottles from restaurants and take them to the recycling place just to get a few dollars for weed. There have been times when I've robbed and beaten up drunk Mexicans as they stumbled out of bars so I could buy weed.

10

BACK TO DAD

At this time, I was also becoming very rebellious towards my mom. She and my stepdad were not getting along at the time either. One day, my stepdad and I got into a heated argument. He got up in my face yelling and spitting. He told me that I was acting like a bitch. My reply was instant and filled with malice, "Look at your own fat ass, bitch!" He immediately grabbed me by the throat and choke slammed me through the door of the closet. As I tried to fight back, he swung and hit me in the eye hard enough to burst a vessel. My eye was both red and swollen for over a month.

The decision was made for me to go live with my biological father. That would allow my mother and stepdad the opportunity to work on their marriage. This was the second time I was sent off to live with my biological father. I stayed with him in Louisiana for about a year.

11

ANGER

A t age 13, I completely broke out of my shell. Up until then, I
was more of a mama's boy. I was shy. Even still, I have always
had a temper. I would get angry at the drop of a dime. Without a
doubt, machoism was the driving force behind my temper. Whenever
people tried to play me or talk down to me, it set me off. Usually, I
rationalized my anger by telling myself that it was someone else's
fault because they were the ones that made me mad.

My mom never tolerated my siblings and I fighting each other. She
always said that if we were angry, to go outside and fight someone on
the streets. I would take her words literally. On numerous occasions, I
would go outside and hit the first person I came across. I never gave a
second thought to the fact that they'd done nothing wrong to me. Or I
would purposely pick a fight. Sometimes I'd grab a bat or stick and
would try to break it on someone. At a young age, I learned that it is a
dog eat dog world. The world is a cruel place. If you don't learn to be
just as brutal, you'll get eaten up quickly. So, I learned.

Admittedly, it is extremely difficult for me to control myself once I'm
angry. Sometimes, it depends on why I'm mad. I remember once

when my little brother cooked Cup Noodles soup in the microwave. As he removed the cup, he spilled the hot water on his arm. I saw the skin shrivel up until the pink meat beneath started showing. My brother screamed and cried in pain, as if he were dying.

I became maniacal and started throwing things around the house. My mother forced me to leave because she couldn't care for my brother, and, at the same time, calm me down. In a state of fury, when I spotted a Hispanic guy on the street, who looked about my size, without comment, I punched him as hard as I could and continued assaulting him until he lay balled up on the ground with blood pouring from his face. In that rage, I didn't realize I was crying while beating on him. Upon my return home, I learned that the police were looking for someone who had beaten a guy until he was unconscious.

My mom asked me why I was so upset and flipped out. I told her it was because my little brother was hurt and I couldn't help him. She assured me that he had hurt himself and I shouldn't be mad.

Later, in conversation, my mother asked me why I looked mad all the time. I realized I didn't know how to express my feelings; well, at least not without my emotions coming out wrong or aggressive. She said, "You can tell people how you feel without becoming upset. Often, in communicating, it's not what you say but how you say it." Once I began to control my anger, my social skills elevated.

12

CRIMINAL MINDED

A t this point in life, I could no longer tolerate being broke, dusty, with old clothes on, and holes in my shoes. I was in high school and getting clowned and talked about just wasn't cool. I was regularly involved in fights. I didn't want to be looked down on, so I began doing everything I could to make money, mostly by stealing. I knew I was committing crimes I but didn't care.

Eventually, I had money to buy better clothes. However, I thought I couldn't tell my mom how I was getting the money. I was scared to get in trouble. That is, until one day, I came home with a pair of $150 Nike shoes. My mom stopped me. I thought she wanted to ask where I had gotten the shoes, but instead, she complimented me, telling me how nice they looked. She also told me she was glad to not see me wearing Chuck Taylor shoes, which were the signature shoes of a lot of gang members back then. Then she spoke again and surprised me, "Let mama hold a hundred dollars." I reached into my pocket and gave her two hundred. She never asked where I got the money, so from then on, every time I committed a crime that got me paid, I would give my mom money for the house.

I even bought groceries. I was just doing what I had to for my family to survive.

I started hanging out with the "fly guys." With them, there was always a competition to see who had the most money or who was the best dressed. We got our money by what we called, "flocking." Flocking is when you break into a house and steal valuables. Each time we flocked, the gains would simply be the luck of the draw. Sometimes we hit it big and sometimes we ended up with nothing. On my first flock, we found a stash of cash and jewelry, along with some expensive alcohol. We sold the jewelry and liquor. All in all, we ended up with twenty thousand dollars. There were four of us, so we each came away with five thousand. I was hooked from that moment on. With flocking, in addition to the big loot, there was less risk of getting caught or using a gun.

I put it to myself to find all the best ways to get paid. I tried selling crack off and on, but honestly, it was too slow for me. I robbed a couple of mom and pop stores in my hood but there wasn't much money in it. I was also told that you don't shit where you sleep. I would see guys riding around in nice cars with shiny rims and cool beats. When I saw guys, I looked for a way to carjack them. I would sell cars to chop shops to bring in some good money.

I learned fast that at any time, things can go wrong so that even I could become a victim. I was fifteen when I became one while I selling crack. Two crackheads asked me if I had anything. I was trying to floss (act) like I was doing big things when all I had was a $50 double up (crackrock with a street value of $50) I was shocked when one of the guys pulled a gun on me while the other one took the dope and the few dollars I had in my pocket. I was furious but there was absolutely nothing I could do.

Another time I was a victim stands out vividly in my mind. I was sitting on the homie Peanut's porch when a crew of crackheads pulled up in a car. I went over and leaned into the car to talk to the passenger and driver. I was showing them the rocks that I had when suddenly the passenger slapped my hand. The rocks flew into the car and they drove off. I felt like a straight sucka.

Peanut told me that to beat a crack head, you had to think like a crack head. With that in mind, I decided not to curb serve, but, instead, I began selling crack from Peanut's backyard.

As I said, dope dealing was too slow for me. I needed to make real money real fast. So, one day, I decided to rob a liquor store with my homie called Charlie Brown. I never did that again because the store clerk chased after us and popped a few shots at us as we ran. I learned my lesson.

The thing I liked most was carjacking. I would catch people getting into their nice cars and rob them at gunpoint. I relished in the feeling of power by taking everything they had. I would take the cars to the chop shop and get a few hundred dollars depending on the make and model.

I made a lot of money doing this, but I heard that if I ever got caught, I could get life in prison for kidnapping so I stopped for a while.

Of all these ways of getting paid, I can say that generally breaking into houses was a success. Plus, I wasn't getting caught. With breaking into houses, I wasn't hurting anybody and I was taking care of my family.

13

EAST COAST CRIPS

My gang is known as the East Coast Crips. We are one of the biggest Crip gangs in Los Angeles. We weren't the biggest in members; however, we have more "clicks" than any other gang. We have the 1st, 59th, 62nd, 66th, 68th, 69th, 76, 89th, 97th, 102nd, 118th, 190th, and 1200 blocks. The numbers represent a street number. My click was 76th. We have 76th street and 76 place. It's all the same gang and neighborhood, it's just that the older homies claim street and us younger guys claim place.

I've grown up in my hood since I was eight years old. I've seen a lot of things going on over the years. I have always heard of the notorious East Coast Crips. I really can't pinpoint exactly what it was that got me hooked on the gang, but in the 90's, the whole khaki and Chuck Taylor look was the fad. I did everything I could to mimic the entire gangsta look.

I lived dead in the center of two rival gang hoods, the Kitchen Crips and the East Coast Crips. Now I had been in the streets since I was thirteen and had been hanging with gang members, even though, at the time, I wasn't part of East Coast. Even still, it was like I was because that's who I hung with on a daily basis. Most of my homies had family members that were from East Coast and that's why they joined. I had no family at that time that was from my neighborhood. Most of my family were Bloods.

I've known people who joined a gang because they had no family of their own so the gang filled a void. As for myself, I had no reason to join other than stupidity. I wanted to be respected and looked up to like the OG's I grew up around. I guess I joined because of the influence of the neighborhood where I was raised and a lot of my friends were already banging.

We used to be in the hood and the homies would joke about putting me on the set, yet I'd always decline. On a daily basis, I was asked by the older homies if I was ready. I never felt truly pressured because regardless if I claimed the gang or not, everybody treated me the same as we all grew up together. I only felt pressure to join East Coast when I would go outside my hood. Other gang members would bang on me and ask me where I was from. It got real when gang bangers started doing body checks on me for gang tattoos. Then, when that wasn't enough, I started getting the question, "Where you live at?" The area you lived in would often reveal gang affinity and be taken as such, regardless if you banged or not. I was chased and got into far too many fights.

What made the decision for me to join East Coast was when a car pulled up along the side of me as I walked to a friend's house. Two Bloods dressed in all red were inside. No words were exchanged, but I noticed a gun in the hand of the guy sitting in the passenger seat. I was gone. I instantly took off running. Before firing at me, I heard one of them yell, "Fuck cheese toast!" (that's how you dissed East Coast).

Once I felt safe from harm, I began to think about the fact that I was getting shot at and wasn't even a gang member. The reality was, I was getting shot at for merely living in the neighborhood I lived in. I was done resisting the gang. If I was going to get shot at for living where I did, I'd represent my hood as an East Coast Crip.

Everybody was shocked when I showed up on the block and asked to be put on the set. I knew I was taking a big step and the decision was one of the biggest of my young life. Yet, I knew what I was getting myself into. These gangstas were the same people I had grown up around and fought before.

When I got jumped on the set, it wasn't any surprise to anyone to see my fighting skills. I was put on (jumped) by my homies Pee Wee and M-Dog. Even though M-Dog and I were about the same size (I was older), I had the most trouble with the little homie Pee Wee. In the midst of punches being thrown, I managed to put M-Dog on his back pockets yet, Pee Wee and I were still going at it. I thought it was over when I hit Pee Wee square in the chin and his eyes rolled back in his head, but then I heard a stampede of feet and saw six or seven of the homies rushing me. I threw a couple of punches until I started getting hit from every direction. I kept telling myself not to hit the ground. I put my back against the wall and covered up as best I could.

Finally, I heard my big homie Woody Loc call all of them off of me. Everybody embraced me and showed me love, except for Pee Wee and M-Dog. Of the three of us, I had the least amount of damage. I ended up with a cut over my top lip. No one, however, could see the lumps under my afro. M-Dog was light skinned, so the bruises on his face were quite prominent. Pee Wee had knots on his head that made his braids come undone.

We sat around mad at each other because everyone was joking and laughing at how I had whooped up both of them up when I was the one getting put on the hood. It was supposed to have been the opposite. I was the one who was to have gotten an ass-kicking. Nevertheless, when the weed was passed around and everyone got to smoking, we got over our anger and focused on getting high.

Now the second part of me getting put on was that I had to go on a mission. I had to find an enemy and shoot him. That night, I don't know if I hit anyone, but I did learn one thing, I loved my hood loyalty.

My big homie Dusty took two of the little homies and me on a mission. The one promise he made us was that he wouldn't leave us. We were jumping fences and running through backyards and true to his words, he was right there with us.

I got my gang name that night. We were smoking weed and drinking when I was asked what my name would be. I wanted to be under my road dog Maniac, so I pushed to be called Baby Maniac. My homie Woody Loc however, wanted me to be called Tiny Woody. One of the founders of my hood, C-Loc, spoke up. He said I needed to have my own name. "Pitch Blacc," he said. We were all high by this time and started laughing. "Naw," he said. "Real talk. You're hella black, but I watch you and you move real nice in the dark." I didn't believe a word C-Loc was saying, but he continued. "Plus, I got a feeling you're gonna be a cold killa, putting nigga's lights out, pitch black." It was like he'd said some deep prophetic shit and everyone shook their heads in agreement. We kept smoking.

I took C-Loc's words to heart because I knew my gang was well known and I needed to live up to it. I felt my hood was the hardest hood in LA.

My mom told me that she realized I wasn't going to be a doctor or a lawyer. She said, "Baby, whatever you do in life, give it your all." So, that is exactly what I did. My hood meant everything to me. I could get anything I wanted. If I wanted drugs, they were there. If I wanted guns or even girls, there they were. Of course, I wanted to earn my own like everybody else. I didn't want to ask for money so I went with the homies whenever it was time to do some dirt.

14

HOMIES

B y this time, my social skills were well up to par. Mostly, my method of being social is to be funny. I was the one in my group of friends who kept everybody laughing and joking. I learned that out of us all, I was the more level headed one. Whenever there was a problem, everyone would come to me because I got along with everyone.

Even though I had lots of friends growing up, two of my main friends were Peanut, whom I mentioned earlier, and Maniac. They were my boys. Peanut was a jokester, like me. He was more animated, however. He was always doing flips and tricks on his bike. Maniac was a straight hard as hell, didn't give a fuck, gangsta. He didn't care about anything. Even though we all had other groups of friends, when we were together, we would hang out, smoke weed all day, and play video games. Yet, while I took to the gang banging with Maniac, Peanut didn't. So, when we were with him, we wouldn't do the gang stuff. Even still, we all committed crimes together.

I don't know if Peanut was the smart one or just scared as hell, because every time we did something, he would try to talk us out of it, or he would choose to be the look-out man. I didn't care. I just wanted to get paid. When I did get into trouble, my mom and dad would think I was letting others talk me into doing crimes. They would tell me not to be a follower, but to be a leader. I have always been one to do exactly what I wanted to do. I have never been a follower. We all just kind of made decisions together. I was, however, the most level-headed.

BABY'S MOMMA

We all had girlfriends. My childhood sweetheart eventually became my wife and the mother of my two beautiful children. Her name is Charlette. We are still married to this day. We've known each other since age eight. Our attraction began at age twelve. I didn't understand relationships back then, so I used to dog her out. I acted like she didn't mean that much to me. I played a role, acting nonchalant as if I didn't care as much about her as I did. Thank God she was in love with me because she hung in there. She is a phenomenal woman and a great mother. She would always want to be around me, but I couldn't have her with me while I was doing dirt.

Charlette tried to keep me away from my gang, but I fought her. I wouldn't listen. For the most part, I took care of her financial needs and wants. She lived a few houses down from me with her grandmother, but like my family, they didn't have much. I showered her with clothes and money because I didn't want her to ask anyone for anything. Plus, she was my girl, so I felt it was my job to provide for her. I grew to love her. I stopped dogging her and spent most of my days with her.

THE PLAN TO KILL DAD

One of the darkest periods in my life was when I was fifteen and, for the third time, went to live with my father. During this period, he was chasing a woman who ended up becoming his fiancé. They were living in Mississippi. He wanted to start a computer business. I wound up living with my dad because, while at my mother's, in Los Angeles, I was charged with burglary. The judge in California was about to put me in California Youth Authority (CYA), prison for minors. My dad sent the judge a letter intervening and asking that mercy be shown and I go to live with my dad rather than be put in CYA. To my great surprise, the judge agreed.

Living with my dad ended up being hell on earth. I lived with the two of them for a little over a year, a year filled with both verbal and physical abuse. The abuse I suffered was from the hands of my father's fiancé.

My dad would travel every week and come home on the weekends. When I was alone with this woman, she was a monster. She would strike me for the smallest of things. Yet, when my dad was around, she would transform and be kind and sweet.

When I told my dad he didn't believe me. His fiancé countered my words by saying that she felt disrespected by me. She said that when she asked me to do something, I would ignore her. I felt she wanted me to instantly drop everything I was doing to rush off and do her bidding. She scolded my father and told him that he was too soft toward me by allowing me to run around and do whatever I wanted to do. The end result of our confrontation was that my dad asked me to respect her and he changed his behavior towards me. His behavior change was all the ammunition she needed. Any time she felt vindictive, she would say something to him and my dad jumped down my throat. He seemed to be going out of his way to please her.

Once, she got mad because I wouldn't wear a pair of pajamas to bed that she had purchased for me. Of course, my dad confronted me. I told him that I was used to sleeping in boxers and a T-shirt. Instead of being understanding, he beat my ass.

Another time, she was going through my stuff and found a pair of thong panties and told my dad. He asked me about the panties and I confessed that I had had sex with a certain girl. His fiancé was furious and told him to beat me. Her justification was that I was too young to be having sex. I didn't understand why my dad would whoop me because he was a ladies' man himself. He was all about getting females. It wasn't until later that he told me that he struck me just to shut his fiancé up. I was advised to hide my things better. I felt betrayed.

During the week when my dad wasn't around, she would do things like slap me in the back of my head if I didn't immediately do something she asked or she would even choke me. She also would continually snatch me by my shirt. When my dad was home, she wouldn't touch me, but she would make him strike for the stupidest of things.

Her abuse became more than I could handle. I couldn't hold it any longer so, one night, I decided to kill both of them. My dad's fiancé came home late and drunk. She usually was back by 6:00 p.m. but that night, she came home around 10:00 p.m. My dad wasn't home at the time. I was asleep when she came into my room and slapped me out of my sleep. She reeked of alcohol. She asked me where the Kool-Aid was. I informed her that it was in the cabinet. She told me to go back to sleep.

I felt like killing her right then and there. Instead, I lay in bed fuming until around midnight. I heard my dad come in. He was talking to her but she didn't respond, so my dad went to bed. Once I knew they were asleep, I took off the leg of a chair and walked into the living room. She was sleeping on the sofa. As hard as I could, I swung the leg down and hit her in the head. I tried to crush her skull. I was going to swing and hit her again, but she woke up screaming. In a panic, I ran out of the house. It was around five in the morning. I had every intent to kill my father as well.

I ended up being arrested and placed in jail. Because of my previous rebellion and lying, no one believed me when I explained how I was being treated. I was elated when I was finally released and saw my mother waiting for me. She had spoken with my dad and his fiancé and convinced them to drop the attempted murder charges. I was released into the custody of my mom. We flew back to L.A.

17

CRIMINAL ENTERPRISING PART ONE

I was sixteen when I came back to Los Angeles from Mississippi. Being again on familiar ground, of course, caused me to start back at doing familiar things. I started back carjacking. It was quick and easy money. I would simply drop the cars off at the chop shop.

One time, two of my homies and I, one was from 20's Crips and the other was from Legend Crips, lied to our moms, telling them that we were staying late for football practice, when really we were going to Hollywood to rob people.

I tried to rob this guy who was getting into his car. He was driving a BMW, so I was sure he had his shit together. I knew he had a pocket full of money. My dumb ass walked up and asked him if he had the time. He glanced over at me and then quickly slammed and locked his car's door. He sped off. I realized that he reacted like that because, first, I had a watch on so I already had access to the time and, second, the butt of my .38 revolver was sticking halfway out of the waistband of my pants.

My Crip homies and I continued to seek out potential victims. Later that night, I sent the homie from 20's to rob a lady for her Lexus. I instructed him on how to do it. I told him to ask her to break twenty dollars. When she looked up, he was supposed to rob her for her purse. At the same time, the homie from Legend and I would be creeping up and jump in her car. I got excited when I heard the lady scream. I told the Legend Crip homie with me to get ready but, to my surprise, the 20's homie ran past us and didn't stop. Confused, we took off after him. We caught up with him a few blocks over. I immediately asked him what he'd gotten. "Nothing," he replied almost out of breath. I didn't understand and asked what happened. He said he asked the lady for change and when she turned around and saw his face, she started screaming. He then got scared and ran. Although I laughed, I also realized that our skin color set us apart in a negative way from everybody else.

18

YOUNG BLACK MAN IN AMERICA

I remember walking to the store once for my mom. I took off through the alleyway because it was faster. I was stopped by two white cops. They pushed me up against the car and searched me without provocation. They were far too rough. One of the cops asked me where the weed was? I told him I didn't smoke. He responded by asking me where the crack house was located. I had no answer. The older of the two called me a nigger and said, "Next time I see your monkey ass, you'd better have some weed."

I knew that cops were crooked, but that was the first time I'd seen it up close and personal. I didn't know if they were serious about the request, but from that point on I tried to keep some weed on me. I began thinking that since the whole country thinks black people are criminals, I shouldn't feel bad about doing crimes.

✖ ✖ ✖

Honestly, I don't believe that being born black in America has had a significant influence on my destiny. My mom once apologized to my older brother and me. My brother asked why she was apologizing. She said, "I brought you boys into this world with two strikes against you." I asked what she meant. She replied, "For one, you're born black. Secondly, you are big." Meaning our weight. She continued, "Those two things place a target on your back."

Now to an extent, I believe this, but at the same time, I know people who grew up in the same neighborhood yet became successful. My skin color may have made people dislike me, but it didn't make my life path. I had the choice and I chose the wrong way. My father showed me a better life and I ran from him. See, my skin color had made people from a different race discriminate against me, but it didn't define my choices.

19

THE SQUARE LIFE

I n my lifetime, I have done a lot of bad things, but also some good. No matter what I did, I felt that I was being the best man I could for my family and myself. I figured that I would be looked at as less than a man if I didn't take care of my family or contribute to my household.

I was seventeen and Charlette was eighteen when we found out that she was pregnant with my firstborn, my son. Honestly, this was the turning point in my life. I ended up going to court on my birthday. When I was fourteen, I was arrested for burglary and placed on probation. On my birthday, I had to go to court and check in.

In court, my stepdad told the judge all kinds of negative things I was doing at home. He also reported that I wasn't going to school. Some of the things he said were lies, but most of it was true.

I was placed under arrest and was about to be sent to California Youth Authority (CYA), but the judge changed his mind and gave me a second chance because he'd found out that I was about to become a new father. He chose to send me to fire camp instead.

There I was, sitting in fire camp kicking myself because I was missing the birth of my son. I wanted to be a father and take care of my responsibilities. Even though I had my mom and stepdad in my life, I kept thinking about what I could do to give my child a better life than I had. There was no question, I wanted to be in my son's life.

Even still, fire camp was one of the best experiences I've ever had. I had to fight because I was a gang banger, but the training and skills I learned made me feel like I could be someone in life.

Another good thing about fire camp was that I earned a few thousand dollars which helped provide for my son. I was in fire camp for a little under a year. My son was two months old when I came home.

The future I saw for myself was getting a good job and a place to live for my child and his mother. Of course, I tried getting a job. I put on suits and went to interviews, and strangely I didn't feel out of place. At the same time, I never actually saw myself living in such a way.

Through the state, I was placed in an adult school where I found a job working at the Staples Center (where the Los Angeles Lakers play). The pay was horrible. I was barely making minimum wage. That wasn't the worst part. The company had all of these taxes and fees. By the time I received my check, I barely had enough to buy baby diapers and infant meal.

Fatherhood had me thinking hard about my life. I pushed away from the streets and tried to tackle going straight, do the right way of living. I even started going to church with Charlette and my son. Even though times were hard, it felt good that I earned money the right way instead of doing crime. Even though the money wasn't enough, it just felt correct doing honest work. My happiest times were with Charlette and my son. I would drive them to any park I could find and we would have a picnic and do the family thing. This also gave me time to escape from the surroundings of the hood for a while.

At work, I never missed a day or showed up late, because I didn't want to miss out on earning any money by not showing up. Then, my car broke down. My broken down car put a significant strain on my ability to make it to my job. It also caused me to think of far quicker ways to get paid, although initially, I rejected those thoughts. My homie Maniac would drive me to and from work and believe it or not, he was actually down for me working and doing the right thing. Even still, I felt like I was a burden to him. Then, I got into it with my stepdad and got kicked out onto the streets. It seemed like everything was going wrong.

Thanks to my hood, I never had to sleep in my car. I bounced around from house to house and this, in turn, placed me back in the center of the gang scene. Plus, I started getting high again. As a result, I went back to doing what I'd always done to survive, crime.

I must admit, the sound of the streets calling me felt good. I heard it's cry loud and clear. All of my homies were glad I was back. After all, I was the one who'd always kept things live in my hood.

20

CRIMINAL ENTERPRISING
PART TWO

O nce, the homie from Legend Crips said that he knew how to jump-start a stick shift car. We found a Honda with a door unlocked. We pushed that car for two blocks trying to start it. I realized that you had to have the car turned on and since we didn't have a key, we were just three idiots pushing a stolen car down the street. We ended up leaving the car in the middle of the road and headed for the bus stop.

I was the only one with any money. I had a dollar. Of course, I was angry because nothing was going the way it should have. I was stressed out. I found a store and asked a smoker who was standing outside to go in and buy a Black and Mild for us. I gave him the dollar I had. When he came back with the change, I couldn't deny him when he asked for it.

Now, at this point, we were all broke as hell sitting at the bus stop in Hollywood, smoking one Black and Mild, when out of nowhere two Hispanic guys walked up and asked if we were selling weed. The three of us looked at each other and read each other's minds. We were about to rob these fools. I asked how much they wanted to buy. One of them said that they only had ten dollars. I was instantly turned off by the idea. We had struck out all night and I didn't want to do no running around for ten dollars. The homie from 20's nudged me as an indicator for me to go ahead and rob the Mexicans, but my attention focused across the street. I noticed a man in a blue Crown Victoria pulling up to the phones at the gas station.

When the guy backed up the car into the parking spot, I didn't think, I reacted. I dashed across the street, leaving the homies and the two Hispanic guys behind. Yelling over my shoulders, I encouraged the homies to catch up with me. By the time I reached the guy, he was standing beside the car stretching. I asked if he had change for ten dollars. He quickly said no, but I was already reaching for my gun. I guess he thought I was reaching for money, so he changed the no to yes. I drew my gun and told him to give me the money. I almost hit him when he peeled two five dollar bills off of the stack of cash to give to me as change. I must have looked extremely frightening to him because before I could utter the words, "Motherfucker don't play with me," he handed me the wad of cash. For a moment, I didn't know what to do. I questioned if I should run, or shoot him. Then I realized that I could just take the car. It wasn't until I jumped in and started the car that the two homies came running across the street and jumped in.

I'm not going to lie, I even bullied them. There ended up being eight hundred dollars. I told them that since they didn't do anything to help, they had to split three hundred between the two of them. I kept five hundred for myself.

I dropped them off and gave the car to one of my Mexican homies, who I later learned got caught with it while trying to fill it up with gas and not pay. He was charged with receiving stolen property. I also learned that the police were looking for a stocky, dark-skinned guy for the robbery.

Soon after that, the cars and rims started coming and with them, a hunger grew inside me for more. I had to do what I had to do to satisfy my cravings.

21

SHERM MADNESS

It was around this time I began to try other drugs. I tried PCP. Most people call it "sherm." It's actually embalming fluid. The first time I smoked a chronic blunt dipped in sherm, I was mostly disoriented and my stomach was upset. One of my homies gave me ginger ale to drink. Once I felt better, I felt nothing. I felt empty.

I didn't experience the high everyone talked about so, of course, I tried it again. This time, I tried smoking it with a cigarette. It was smooth. I'd never felt so good. I was on cloud nine. I felt like a mack, like a true player. I felt as if I could talk the panties off of any woman I spoke to.

This feeling, of course, led me to try sherm again. I was chasing after that smooth feeling. We went to a party and I was not myself. I was dancing with every girl I laid eyes on. I'm no drinker, but that night I was drinking every drink I got my hands on. I don't even know how I made it home, but the next day I woke up in bed with my girlfriend.

This was around the time when one of my big homie's little brother was killed by Mexicans. The boy was only twelve years old. He was walking home from the park and was shot over twenty-five times with an AK-47 assault rifle. He had to have a closed casket funeral. This was a turning point. I snapped. I got into the gang life even more so than usual.

The killing caused a lot of us to take shifts going out and shooting up Mexican gangs. I stayed in a furious state of mind when it came to certain gangs. I could be happy and thinking about my son, but once I saw one of the rivals, I instantly became enraged. All I could think about was how they had killed an innocent kid.

One day, I was in my hood and my homie told a group of us that the rivals were hanging out in their neighborhood. Maniac was with me. He and I had done a lot of things together. So much so, that shooting and killing had become like a game to us. We would actually argue on the way to our rival's hood about whose turn it was to do the shooting.

This particular day was like any other. We argued and I was the winner because we were using his car and he had to drive. Maniac kept his gun in a stash spot behind the car's radio. I reached into it grabbing the gun while not realizing that I had accidentally hit the eject button for the clip. When we pulled up to our rival's location, before they could see me and get the chance to run away, I was hanging out the window with the gun in my hand. I aimed for the guy's chest. I popped off and ended up hitting him in the stomach. As he fell, his homie ran. I pointed the gun at the guy's head. When I pulled the trigger, nothing happened. We sped off. When I looked down, I noticed the clip had fallen into my lap. To this day, I don't know if the guy I shot died, but I do know that if it wasn't for the clip falling out, there would have been multiple bodies lying on the ground.

✖ ✖ ✖

The fourth and final time I used PCP, I was in a gang allies'
hood hanging out and smoking weed dipped in sherm. I got a
call from one of my homies informing me that there was a hood meeting. I was high out of my mind. PCP enhances whatever mood you're
in. During this time, I was doing a lot of partying and having quite a
lot of shoot-outs. Also, around this time, I lost my grandfather. I was
holding a lot of pain and anger inside. Finally, to gang violence, I had
lost three close homies with whom I had grown up. I needed to retali-
ate. I relished being in the bottomless pit of street life.

When I got to my hood, my homies were out deep. The meeting was
about who in the hood wasn't putting in work. Now even though I
had lived in the hood and was very active with my gang banging, the
PCP had me turned up even more than normal and I went into a
rage. I started yelling at the homies, calling them "marks" and saying
who was and wasn't putting in work. I was calling out anybody I
thought was scared to put in some work. The next thing I knew, I was
barking orders and demanding that the homies get in my car to go kill
some Mexicans. I wasn't surprised when my orders were being
followed.

Driving around, we spotted two Mexican gang members walking
along with two females and three kids. I ordered the homie in the
passenger seat, (I won't name him), to shoot them. He told me no
because they were with children. I have never felt so evil in my entire
life. I started screaming at the top of my lungs. "Fuck them kids, cuz!
They killed the homie's little brother!" By this time, we had passed
the guys and I had to circle back around the block. I was known for
being irascible. At this point, I was irate. "Fuck it cuz, give me the
gun! Imma kill 'em myself", I shouted. Someone else in the car (no
names will be mentioned) spoke up letting me know that I couldn't
be the shooter because I was the one driving the car. I was furious. I
drove back around the block and the Mexican guys must have recognized my car after we had passed the first time. They had sent the

two females and the kids to walk ahead of them. As we passed, I told the homie to shoot them. Once I saw one of them hit the ground, we sped off.

Back in the hood, we bragged about the work we'd put in. When I was home and finally sober, I thought about what had happened. I told myself I would never do PCP again. It put the devil in me. I couldn't believe I was about to kill some kids. Now I have done a lot of things, bad things, but being a child killer is not me. Yet in spite of my moment of regret, I was still turned up and wanted revenge for the death of the homie's little brother. All of us were intent on revenge, so we continued to handle our business.

It got to the point where neither side cared if the kids got involved or not. I had to keep my reputation high, so I went on mission after mission just to be doing something. It was all a blur.

At this point, I had rekindled my relationship with my mom and step-dad, but honestly, I really didn't care about much so long as my son was taken care of. And of course, I cared that I kept money in my pocket.

22

MY CRIME

D eep down inside, I knew that the mixture of robbing, stealing, and gang banging would eventually catch up to me, so while I had money in my pockets, I gave my baby's mama money to save and I bought my son clothes. I would buy the clothes a few sizes too big. My family thought I was crazy for doing so, but I wanted to be sure that he would have something just in case I wasn't around.

To be honest, I didn't put too much thought into getting caught because I was doing too much and getting away with it. Dwelling on going to prison was not something I did. Nonetheless, I figured if I did, it would be for robbing and not gang banging because robbing was what I did most.

The morning after the hood meeting was the day the crime for my current incarceration took place. We had an M16 that we needed to take to one of the homies that was from 62. (It's pronounced six-deuce.) We didn't have any plans on putting in any work or going on any missions. We were simply returning the gun. I was driving my Caprice Classic. I never shot out of that car. A Mexican gang member either recognized me or he may have known my car. He and his homies opened fire on us, but one of my partners was able to get off some shots with the M16. I hit a few corners to get out of the line of fire; they tried to cut me off a few blocks down the street. I didn't realize I was heading straight into a blood gangs hood. The Hispanic guys that were pursuing us actually lived in the area. I heard more shots and realized that they had us cornered yet a few more bursts from the M16 my homie had sent everyone running. The chaos allowed us to escape. In the midst of all the shooting, I noticed one of the Hispanic guys fall to the ground. I didn't look back.

Somehow, the police had an idea of what area we were in. They caught up to us coming out of a store in the 62nd East Coast hood. None of us, by that time, had any guns. In spite of this, the police arrested everyone with a white T-shirt on. A witness had given a description of my car. Everyone was eventually released except for me because of my car.

The police found seven .223 shell casings at the shooting location along with seven .9mm casings. However, at the murder scene, they only found one .9mm casing. Inside my car, they found three .223 casings.

Even though I was not the shooter, I was found guilty because I was driving the car. I know in my heart that if we had not had the M16, we would have been killed. I was sentenced to fifteen years to life, with the possibility of parole. I received sixteen years in enhancements for a total of thirty-one years to life.

23

PLOT TWIST

E ast Coast Crips was my life. I lived for my hood. I gave it my all. I was completely loyal to it. Until fighting this case, I didn't realize that I had already built a reputation. I was going hard when all I had to do was just kick back. When my name came up, it held its own weight. I rank my gangsterism at an eight and my gang, East Coast Crips, a most definite ten.

In spite of this, here I sit. I'm in prison for a gang murder. I was locked up at the time when I found out that Charlette was pregnant with my daughter, Ahniya. The sad thing is, I have never been home for my baby girl, and I only got to be with my son for nine months.

I thank God every day for Charlette because she was strong enough to stand by me and she keeps the kids in my life. Even though from behind bars I watch them grow up, I am counted amongst the blessed. In 2015, Charlette agreed to marry me and become my wife. We work hard to keep our family together and our kids going down the right path.

✖ ✖ ✖

One of the bitterest pills I've ever had to swallow was being locked up when my mother passed away. She died from kidney failure just like my grandmother, Queenie, did. At the time, I felt as if I wanted to die also, but my children kept me strong. I was twenty-five years old.

My mother's death caused me to run head first into a wall of reality. I was wilding out and getting into all sorts of trouble in prison, but when she died, it caused a fundamental shift in me. I grew up.

One memory I hold as sacred as a religious person does her deity. See, I never finished high school, but, while in prison, I obtained my GED. Getting my GED felt as if I was working a job all over again but it also felt great accomplishing something. Even though I was confined when I obtained my GED, imprisonment in no way diminished the joy.

My mother was alive and got to see me achieve this. Just hearing her voice telling me how proud of me she was, made me feel as proud as I did on the day my son was born.

✘ ✘ ✘

However, the proudest moment in my life came on the day that I stopped worrying or caring about what other people thought about me. It happened in 2016. That was the day I allowed Lauren to be born. I say this because I stopped hiding who I honestly am: I am transgender.

Obviously, by my story, one can see that I did not live my life on the streets as a transgender, but I have known since the age of ten that I was different, born in the wrong body. I hid who I was. I let the pressure of what others, mainly my father, would think of me keep me from being myself. Even though I had the desire to be a woman, I didn't want to disappoint my father or even worse lose his love for me.

As I mentioned before, my father was a strong male figure in my life. He was one of those macho men who thought everything was a test of manhood.

I was ten when we had an incident at home when some female panties popped up in our laundry. My father went crazy, questioning my brother and me about why panties were in the laundry. He was furious and asked if one of us was "gay." I will never forget the angry look that filled his eyes. That still wasn't what caused me to hide myself and my emotions.

My brother lied and told my dad that he had a girl over and she must have left the panties. A look of relief came over my dad's face. The words he uttered are what kept me hiding for twenty years. He said that he was sorry for accusing us and that his biggest fear in life was that one of his sons end up gay. His words inscribed in me great anxiety that rung in my mind for years. I could never tell my dad that I actually stole the panties from one of his girlfriends.

Even still, not even my father's persona stopped me from feeling like I should have been born female. I did everything my dad wanted. I played sports and lifted weights. I dated girls and even lied to my father about having multiple girlfriends just so he would be proud of me. I lusted after women, but in truth, I was actually envious of them. I couldn't shake my father's words, so I went on to have two beautiful children. Now make no mistake, I have no regrets about my children being born. However, I do wish I could have been strong and been the person I felt I have always been. Maybe I would have saved myself a lot of pain and grief. I probably wouldn't even be in prison now. It's a hard thing to not care what others think of you. Eventually, I had a breaking point as I was unhappy because I was faking about who I indeed am.

All my life while committing crimes and gang banging, I still knew that I was Lauren, but I became extremely skilled at hiding her. For example, I would be chilling with the homies in the hood and underneath my clothes, I would be wearing some panties. I even went on a few missions wearing thong panties. Never once did I give consideration that if I got caught and went to jail, my secret would be revealed. Hell, I'd even dress up in women's clothes while locked in my room.

✗ ✗ ✗

For a long time, while incarcerated, I hung around the transgenders. Everybody thought I wanted to get with one when, in truth, I wanted to be one. I had a friend who was feeling like me and he found the courage to begin his transformation into "she." I thought that I could never make such a move because I was married, plus a lot of people knew me and looked up to me as that vicious gang banger, Pitch Blacc. Inside, I was hurting beyond measure, so much so that I decided to speak with a psychologist about how I felt and how exhausted I was with hiding myself.

I was eventually diagnosed with Gender Dysphoria and placed on hormones. I didn't realize how easy and fast things would change for me. My entire life, I acted like a man, yet soon after taking hormones, people began noticing the changes and would tell me that they couldn't picture me acting like a guy. My facial features softened and my breasts grew. People started treating me like the woman I am.

✗ ✗ ✗

Every transitioning woman has her own story about the things she has been through, but so far, I'm happy to say, I have not experienced too much negativity. I built a reputation for myself and I believe that my reputation, along with the fact that I am in here for murder, has played a significant factor in why I am treated with respect. Being Pitch Blacc has helped a lot.

Plus, I treat everyone with respect. I have always been told that I carry myself with respect. I don't try to fit in with people, I just do me.

I still go to the basketball court and play ball with the guys. Of course, there are times when I get weird looks and even a few laughs. That lasts until the ball is in my hands and I cross a guy over. Then, everyone looks at me as a girl who can hoop.

So far, all of my gang member family I've run into still show me love and respect. I've even been flirted with by some of my homies. I have had only one negative incident with a gangbanger. He was my homie named Bam. He was from my old hood. He had a problem with me changing. Now, even though I have changed physically and somewhat mentally, I still have that thug mentality. I don't allow anyone to get over on me.

There was talk on the yard that Bam had said some foul words about me now being Lauren. Other homies that know how I am, quickly sent word to Bam letting him know that I was looking for him so that we could address the issue. He sent me a kite (note) explaining himself and telling me that he didn't mean any disrespect. He went on to state that it was hard for him to understand my sudden change. He reminded me that we were comrades from the streets and that we didn't see this kind of change in our hood. He ended by saying that he felt as if he had lost a soldier, but that if I was happy, then he was happy for me.

When we were face to face, I let him know that he didn't lose a soldier and that I was still me. All the thugging we'd done, was still inside me. He gave me a hug and we are on good terms.

Recently, during a visit with my dad, my wife, and my kids, I revealed how I now look to them. Now, they had spoken to me on the phone about my transition, but they were shocked when they saw me. All of them said that I look like my mom.

I know that I am lucky because everyone has accepted me for who I am, including my dad. My dad told me he didn't remember the things he'd said to me all those years ago, and that he was sorry that he had. My dad said that he wished I would have told him how I felt a long time ago.

I know that if I had been Lauren on the streets, I would have hung around a different crowd. I would have had different friends. I am just glad I found myself now because I know some people never honestly find themselves.

I do regret that my mom never got the chance to meet her other daughter, me. I know she would still have loved me just the same.

Honestly, I have to say, I blame no one for my involvement in crime. I am a smart individual, raised to do the right thing, but I chose to do wrong. I couldn't wait and work for the things I wanted like most people do. I fell for what the streets showed me.

Yes, I had jobs and respected the decency of honest money, and even felt good earning it, yet something inside of me made me lust for more. To satisfy that lust, I did terrible things to get what I wanted faster.

Even still, I know the things I have gone through have made me who I am today. It is all for the good because at one point in time, I was indeed becoming a wicked-hearted person. I was surviving and I refused to be looked at as weak or a victim. Yes, I wish I could have accomplished more positive things on the streets, but I can say that I know my own self-worth now. I know I am capable of great things. If I could change my life path, I would most definitely remove from my history getting a life sentence, yet I know how I lived. Still, I do regret cheating myself of the opportunity to be in my children's lives. Even so, I cannot stop writing my own story.

II
———————

LAUREN

24

PIGTAILS

I was ten when I realized that I felt different about myself. By that, I mean I felt unsettled about being a male. Within me, in my soul and in my spirit, something told me that I should have been born female. I guess at that age, I did not fully understand the in-depth difference between the sexes, but I did know that deep inside of me, I was the opposite of what was present on the outside.

I know that these feelings did not arise because I was a mama's boy and my mom catered to me as if I was her daughter instead of her son. I know that these feelings arose because for as long as I can remember, I have been intrigued by the femininity of women.

Everything about women captivates me. I love the way women move, their curves, and shape, everything. I know that I was meant to be one as well.

As I say this, I believe that Lauren developed even before I turned ten. I think I began to feel my femininity as young as 3 or 4.

I am the second child my mother birthed. First, there was my big brother, then me. For three years after being born, I was my mom's baby. As I grew, the closer my mother and I became. She always held me close and centered me in her life. She took care of me, no matter what.

I remember having very long hair because my mom never cut it. She would just let it grow. She always used to bomb it (straighten) and keep it up. I recall how she also would put my hair in pigtails just like they did with the little girls.

Even when my little sister was born, my mom still had me on her hip. I think she picked me up more so than she did my sister who was only a few months old at the time. My mom would kiss and caress me as one does a daughter.

I see clearly in my mind a photo of my mom holding me in front of our apartment in the Pueblos. I remember when we took the photo. I cannot remember what happened before or even after the picture, but I do know that it was my brother who snapped it.

My mom had me cradled in her arms. My feelings from that exact moment have never left me. I felt loved and spoiled. I felt completely safe in my mother's arms. I was around five years old. I was big. I remember that my feet reached down past my mom's knees, yet she still held me like I was her baby; like I was her daughter.

From my mother, all I knew at that age was affection. Mostly I received love and tenderness from my mom. She did not expose me to the roughness that one would associate receiving from a father to a son.

I was around eight when my mom and I were talking about me as an infant. I had never actually seen a photo of me as a toddler, and I wanted to know why.

As we spoke, it looked like my mom was in a deep trance. She stared into my eyes and began to share with me her memories of the two of us together. As she did, her eyes sparkled. She mentioned how much she missed me walking up to her with my little sippy cup and in my baby's voice, asking her if we could share my juice. At that moment, I felt closer to her than ever.

I genuinely believe that the way my mother sheltered, protected, and nurtured me encouraged the development of Lauren.

The memory I have that confirms my thinking is of my mother and me talking. I asked her how many kids she wanted to have. She told me three. At the time, there was already three of us. I listened further.

She envisioned having a boy first, then a girl. She said that she would accept the third child no matter what sex the child would be.

I asked why not have a girl first and she explained that she had wanted a son first so that her second child, her daughter, would have a big brother to look up to and to protect her.

That was the first time that I can remember wishing that I had been born a girl. Not because I felt that being born a boy disappointed my mother, but because I wanted my mom to have her wish come true.

When my mom finally hugged me, I felt as if she knew or felt that Lauren was inside of me. My mom knew that inside, she had a daughter. I never looked at those times with my mom as anything other than bonding. I now know that those moments were more. They planted the seeds of my femininity.

25

BOY IN THE HOOD

A s I have said before, at the age of ten, my mind couldn't fully understand and sort all of my feelings, so I held my feelings inside and refused to speak on them. I felt that if I mentioned my feelings, I would be viewed as an outcast. I could not talk to anyone. Plus, you have to understand my environment. I did not know anyone who spoke about having a same-sex attraction or an identity conflict.

Plus, my father's words, as I have said before, kept ringing in my mind. When he said that his biggest fear was that one of his boys end up being gay, his words effectively silenced my voice. That voice remained quiet for twenty years. The thought of losing my father's love was devastating. It shrouded me in shame.

Growing up in my neighborhood, you did not see boys with boys. That was out of the question. I have always been taught that boys only had sex with girls. When my homies and I would all hang out, joking and clowning around, there was a lot of homophobic talk. Plus, religion taught that homosexuals would suffer eternally in hell. Thus, I did not show any signs of femininity because it was forbidden within my family and culturally.

Even at a young age, the desire to be who I am would surface. I recall times when I would sneak around in my room wearing female underwear. I would strut around and sway my hips as I had seen women do. These were movements from the woman within me, yet those feelings and forces were not strong enough to move me past my fears. To live up to the image of being a boy, I did what boys are supposed to do.

26

SEX ON MY 13TH BIRTHDAY

M y first sexual experience was with the girl who ended up later in life being my wife and the mother of my two beautiful children.

I remember our first time like it was yesterday.

It happened on my 13th birthday. As previously stated, Charlette and I had known each other since age 8 and became romantic when I was twelve. Charlette is a year older than me. At age 12, I ended up having to live with my dad, so Charlette and I ended up being apart from each other for nearly a year. During that year, we kept in touch by phone. When I finally came back to Los Angeles, we both knew that the flames between us were still there. It felt as if we had never been apart.

I wanted to spend my birthday with her and no one else. It is funny because we did not plan to have sex on that day, it just happened. However, I remember that in the days leading up to my birthday, we were kissing and groping each other. The sexual tension just seemed to build.

The night before my birthday, we talked on the phone until 11:00 p.m. or so. Everyone at my house was asleep, so I asked if she wanted to sneak over. When Charlette arrived, we picked a spot on the living room floor where we laid a blanket down. We lay together feeling good, talking, and touching on each other. Somehow, we ended up naked. She was acting all shy and seeming like she had no idea what to do. Now by this time I had seen porno movies, so I acted like I was grown and knew how to handle my business. I quickly learned that I did not know a thing.

I had Charlette get on her knees in the doggie style position with me behind her. I started trying to push up inside of her, yet nothing was happening, except for me rubbing my penis up and down between her butt cheeks. I started sweating as if I were doing something, like I was putting in some serious work, but I did not hear her moaning as the women did in the porno movies. Getting worried, I leaned over and whispered in her ear. "Is it in?" I did not know what else to do. "I don't know." She whispered back.

Looking back at my antics makes me laugh. I thought that I was some kind of stud, but I was just a confused kid.

I recall some of my big brother's friends talking about having sex and how good it felt. They always spoke on how warm a girl's pussy was on the inside. I kept trying to put my penis inside of her because I did not feel anything warm. I do not know how long this went on.

I suddenly heard her suck in a lot of air and moan. That was when I felt the warmth of her and her muscles pulled me in. In my mind, I said, "Damn, this shit is warm. "I started pumping in and out of her, mimicking what I had seen in the movies. By this time, the clock on the oven read past midnight, so officially it was my 13th birthday.

I thought I was handling my business and doing something big. Every few pumps, I slid out of Charlette and had to push myself back in. It wasn't until later that I learned that slipping out of a girl during sex was considered a bad thing and that it meant that your dick was not large enough.

I wasn't too bothered, however, for two reasons: first, she never complained that my dick was too little whenever she had seen or held it; secondly, I felt as if I was supposed to be a woman anyway. The only reason I was having sex with a girl was because I was supposed to. Now even though I had gotten aroused by women, I still felt like a girl on the inside.

I often masturbated while wearing panties. I would also stick my finger inside my anus and act like I was a girl having sex. I would moan as a woman does.

27

HORNY

For years, I would not even dare to look at a guy the way girls look at guys. So, I kept my secret fantasies in my bedroom. Eventually, I found and even made objects to stick inside of me.

I admit I loved the feeling of something sliding inside my anus. I just had no idea of who or where to go to experience the real thing. I longed to know that pleasure. I was hungry for that type of sex. Because of my fear, again, I chose to stay with my homemade toys.

There is no question that I was still confused about my inner feelings. I did not know how to choose between my feelings for girls and my sexual desires to feel a boy inside of me. Eventually I chose the safer way and stuck with women. I justified it by thinking it was what I had been taught to do anyway.

Also, there was a different side of me that knew that I was not attracted to guys like I was to girls. I did not want a boyfriend; I just wanted to know the feeling of anal sex. I thought it not an easy thing to find a guy to experiment with, and I can say that I honestly did not try to find one.

28

THE FIRST BLOW JOB

I t was not until my early twenties and while I was in jail fighting
my case, that I started getting strong urges to be with a guy. It
seemed like every time I got horny, the stronger and longer those
urges came. Once I had masturbated and busted a nutt, those urges
would go away. That is until I found myself aroused again.

As I said, I believed it was wrong to have sexual thoughts for men, at
least that is what I was told growing up, so no matter what I was
craving for sexually, I would not allow myself go there. I could not
mentally get past my inhibitions.

I did not realize that my denial of self was creating even more block-
ades to Lauren, who was fighting to be released, to come forth. I was
building the bars to the internal cage that held her in. I kept her
shackled with my fears.

Also, at some point, I do not know when, I developed an idea, which
now I consider absurd, that if I did have sex with a guy, he could not
be black. I felt that if I had sex with a black man, I would be disre-

specting and disgracing my race. I would be a stain on what it meant to be a black man.

Somewhere within me, I justified that if I did have sex with a guy and he was not black, I would not be a disgrace to my people.

I ended up having my first sexual encounter with a skinny, nerdy looking, Asian guy. At the time, I shared a cell with five other inmates. He entered the cell looking frightened; in fact, he was trembling with fright.

I am not sure if my attraction to him was because of the woman inside of me wanting to protect and nurture or the building sexual urges and sexual frustrations inside of me seeing an opportunity for release. Whatever the reason, I figured that I could get to know him and maybe try sexual things with him without anyone finding out about it. In truth, it may have been a little bit of both reasons.

It did not take long for the Asian guy to realize that because of my gang ties and my ruthless reputation, I was respected and even feared. As a result, he started sticking close to me. I guess, in a way, I used my name as a gateway for sex. I never forced him, or have forced anyone for that matter, but what I did was leverage the fears he had.

There are countless crazy stories about the LA County Jail. Stories of inmates being raped, beaten, and even killed. There are rival gang fights all of the time. The officers are dirty and will kick your ass over nothing. It is a real madhouse. Plus, there were not many Asians there either, so he had no real crew for protection or to hang around. Also, he did not have money for canteen (the jail store.)

One night, we stayed up late playing cards. Once everyone went to sleep, I started asking him questions about why he did not leave the cell much. I questioned if he was scared. He admitted to me that he was. He did not want to get beaten up. I told him not to worry. I would make it my business to protect him. Then I asked a question to which I already knew the answer. I asked if he had any family taking care of him. He kept it honest and said no. All of a sudden, I do not know why, my demeanor grew very shy, so much so that I could not vocalize what I wanted to say. I quickly took out a pen and a piece of paper. I wrote on it that if he allowed me to suck his dick, I would not let anyone hurt him and that when the store came around, I would make sure that he had all the things he needed. I also wrote at the end that if he did not want to let me suck his dick, he did not have too. Shyly, I handed him the paper. I do not think I had ever been as nervous as I was in that moment. I watched in anticipation and fear as his facial expressions went through several changes. I had no idea if they were good or bad thoughts. He looked around and saw that everyone was asleep. I was both shocked and pleased when he suddenly leaned back on the bunk and pulled out his dick. In my mind, I could hardly believe that it was about to happen. I was about to wrap my lips around a real dick for the first time.

I quickly slid down to the floor and placed my mouth over the head of his short, fat penis. As soon as my tongue touched his dick, it felt so smooth,

I instantly knew that I was in love with the feel and was going to love sucking dicks.

Not sure of what to do, I again relied on what I had seen in porno movies. Also, I sucked him the way I liked being sucked on. Before I knew it, I was slurping and popping my lips up and down on his dick. I was in a trance. I was in heaven.

I did not realize how loud I was until one of our cellmates moved and rolled over. Even still, I did not want to stop. The Asian guy had to push my head off of his lap because I was making too much noise. Everyone was waking up. He quickly tucked himself into his boxer shorts and got into his own bed.

It was hard for me to fall asleep that night. I ended up laying wide awake all night. I could not believe that I had done it nor could I believe how much I liked it. I had a real Jones to get back to it. I had never been so horny in my life. I wanted to do it again, but he had gone to sleep.

The next morning I was called out of the cell early to attend my scheduled court date. All day, I thought on what had happened the night before. When I got back to the cell, everyone went out for recreation except for the Asian and me.

It is crazy when I think back because there I was, this big, black gangsta, yet the moment the cell door closed, I recall looking to him with female desire. I don't know if it was Lauren coming out of me, but I sashayed my hips like a woman as I walked to him. That walk happened naturally. I felt all sexy and seductive. I felt alive.

I asked him a question, and in the middle of his response, I interrupted and quickly asked if we could finish what we had started. Without hesitation, he pulled down his pants and laid on my bunk. I was instantly on him.

This time I did not hold back yet, knowing that I had time, I did no rushing. I slurped and popped as loud as I could. I took my sweet time savoring and relishing in his taste. I inhaled his scent and enjoyed the feel of his body. I took my time moving my head around in circles and up and down on him. At the same time, I allowed my tongue to lick every inch of his dick.

Before I knew it, he started moaning and moments later, without warning, he came in my mouth. I tasted my first drop of cum. I did not know what to do. I tried to swallow it as it flowed from him, but he shot it in the back of my throat. I ended up spilling it out of my mouth. Being that it was my first time, I had not yet mastered the art of giving head.

Eventually, I learned that I had to slide my mouth to the head of the penis just as the person is about to cum. This technique allows me to swallow it without spilling a single drop.

I will never forget the light buttery taste of his cum. As a lady, I took a soapy towel and washed him up before everyone came back. I felt great, but I also wanted more. I wanted to go further and feel a dick inside of me. Plus, I could hardly wait to get my next chance to suck another dick.

When the other guys returned to the cell, we were sitting on my bunk playing cards, and acting like nothing out of the ordinary had happened. I did everything I could think of to avoid any form of suspicion.

I do not know how the conversation got started, but one of the cellies, an older Mexican guy who barely spoke any English, began talking to another guy in Spanish. The other dude started laughing and attempted to translate into English what was said.

I could not fully understand his words, but I quickly got the gist as he started making hand gestures indicating someone's head bobbing up and down. There was no mistaking his meaning.

In a millisecond, the sexy lady I was feeling on the inside disappeared. She retreated deep within my soul much quicker than she had surfaced. I felt mortified and thoroughly embarrassed. I felt utter shame.

As a result, I reacted and did the only thing I knew to do when I found myself in a bind. I roared up like I was King Kong and tried to rush and attack the old man. There was no way that he was going to get away with embarrassing me by putting all of my business out in front of everyone. I was threatening to beat the hell out of him. Somehow, I was held back.

Even to this day, I can hear his words saying, "I see da suckie suckie." There was no doubt that when he had rolled over the night before, he saw me sucking the Asian guy's dick.

As if a guardian spirit was bailing me out of the situation, suddenly the door to the cell popped open. The correctional officers started calling out the names of the people transferred to another part of the jail. To my surprise, and relief, they called everyone's name except for mine.

Immediately, I told myself that I would never do that again yet, as soon as everyone left, my sexual urges and thoughts came back in full force. It only took the next batch of cellmates arriving before I was back to being my old horny self.

29

POLITICS

I had a few more sexual encounters while in the county jail, yet I never went all the way. That did not happen until I came to prison. At that time, I was still struggling with the thought of messing with a guy of my race. My conflicting thoughts really bothered me and I found them hard to shake.

In the county jail and on the streets, I heard about racism in prison but it took me coming to prison to learn the politics that underline it. Racism and racial segregation are pervasive in prison.

One rule is that everyone cells up with someone of his race. The cells we sleep in are two-manned cells. For me, it was hard because Lauren started resurfacing and popping in and out of my daily life. As she did so, my sexual cravings grew, almost to the point where I could not control them.

As said, I had not yet experienced penetration with a man and I was dying to try. At the same time, I did not want anyone to know that I desired to be a woman, and not just that, but to be someone's woman.

It was tough for me to expose my sexual longings and budding feminity because I did not want to ruin my reputation or worse, not be accepted because of my struggles.

Even still, although I acted like a regular guy, I found myself hanging around the feminine guys or the transgenders. I wanted so badly to become one myself. I desperately wanted just to be myself.

I figured that I would find a transgender whose male organs were still functional, and use her to experiment with sexually. That did not work out in my favor because all of the transgenders I got involved with were straight bottoms. Meaning they did not penetrate their lovers but were strictly penetrated.

At the time, I had not come across a transgender that was a "gun-slinger." That is a term we use for a transgender who gets penetrated yet also penetrates her men as well.

Some people might say that I am crazy because I had no problem being involved with a transgender, yet it was so difficult for me to open up and be myself. I guess image is a powerful thing. With mine on the line, I figured that as long as I was the man in the relationship and doing the fucking, and not the one getting fucked, my actions would not be looked on by other blacks as a bad thing.

Now I know plenty of cis-gendered people may say that if you mess with someone whose born a man, even if she is now a trans woman, then you are gay. They will frown upon your actions. In the gay community, as long as you are the top, "the man," in the relationship, you are not looked upon as gay. Thus, it is easier for others to accept the man who gives over the man who receives.

30

WILD CHILD

I had a Crip homie who was having problems with his cellmate; the two of them were not getting along. He is the man with whom I first experienced same-sex intercourse. For the sake of preserving his identity, I will call him Wild Child.

Wild Child was a fighter and always down for whatever. He also was openly gay. I had wanted to move in with him for a long time but never took any actions to make it happen. I did not want people to start any rumors or even question if I was getting fucked by a man.

Secretly I started writing letters to Wild Child and sharing with him how I felt. I even told him the sexual things I wanted to try. I also let him know that I did not want my business being spoken on by anyone.

I told him about how I would secretly wear panties on the streets and how I felt as if I should have been born a girl. I confessed my deepest secrets to him including how badly I was feeling, but I also knew that I was not ready to fully come out.

I felt gladdened that Wild Child was just like me, with the exception that he did not hide his identity or his sexual preferences. I was thrilled as, for the first time in my life, I had someone with whom I could confide. I was able to learn his thoughts on my feelings.

I began to no longer feel alone or weird for having my inner, female self. Because I had never had anyone to talk to, I had vigorously developed the psychological belief that I had to be a weirdo.

Such a thought may seem strange because I know that there are transgenders all over the world. There are perhaps even millions of them. However, I had never seen one on the streets or anywhere near my neighborhood. In fact, I had never known a gay person, so my feelings were not normal to me.

We ended up using his cell situation to bring about moving in together. The word was that the police had moved him in my cell, so there was not much speculation and no one talked about us. At the same time, it did not take long for talk to happen because everyone knew that I messed around with the transgenders.

Most of the jokes, talk, and speculations, to my relief, were centered around me being the one fucking Wild Child. No one thought that I would be the one on the other end of a dick. Man, if only these walls could talk. They would have some passion driven adventure stories to tell.

Both Wild Child and I penetrated each other, but, mostly, I was the one who was on the receiving end, and I loved it. I played the girl role when we were in the cell, but as soon as our door opened and we walked outside, we walked around like two regular guys.

I loved that when I was with him, I could completely be myself. I walked around in thongs and booty shorts, and I never once worried about being judged. Also, Wild Child loved that I played the girl's role.

Our first time happened when he first moved into the cell. As soon as the door closed behind him, we were all over each other like flies on shit. Our hands groped each other as we both stripped from our clothing. I became even more excited when I saw that Wild Child was wearing a homemade thong just as I was.

Wild Child is shorter than me, but I won't lie, when I saw what he was packing between his legs, it had me more than a little concerned. He showed a 9 1/2 inch dick on soft. It was both fat and heavy. I was relieved to see that when he grew hard, it did not grow any longer; it just became stiff while the size stayed the same. Wild Child must have perceived my apprehension and observed the concern on my face, because I was thinking, "Damn, I can't take that monster." He assured me that he would not rush or hurt me. He promised that he would take his time.

To this day, I thank him for that. I thank him for everything.

He taught me how to keep myself up and make myself attractive and sensual. He was the one who taught me everything I know about cleaning myself. He even showed me a few little tricks in the bedroom that I use even now.

Even though Wild Child was my first sexual partner with whom I tried everything, when we separated, I was left with this craving to want to experience even more men. Being that Wild Child's penis was so big, I felt as if I never really got the chance to enjoy the penetration as I wanted too.

Wild Child could not just slide inside of me and pound away because it would have caused me far too much pain. As a result, he always did it to me slowly. I wanted to see how it would feel to have a man just let go and have his way with me. I wanted to let him pound away and throw caution to the wind; to let him take me doggie style and hard.

Wild Child and I had a lot of sex, yet each time we did, it felt as if it was the first time. It always took him about thirty minutes to get inside of me, and once he had, everything hurt. He taught me how to relax my anal muscles and open up. Nevertheless, even with his coaching his size still caused me pain. Wild Child was just too damn big.

His penis size never turned me off or made me want to stop. He would flip me this way, then that way until he was usually on top of me with my legs over his shoulders or my legs bent up to where they damn near touched my head. I loved it when we were in that position. But, it seemed like every time we finally got him all the way inside of me, and it no longer hurt, he would be cumming. I always thought, "Damn, just when it started feeling nice." I was disappointed and left with a craving. I was left unsatisfied. Even so, I like to think that he came so quickly because I have some "real good-good," as we like to say.

31

MY SPIRIT IN CONFLICT

I did not think that I would ever be brave enough to let Lauren out completely. I had seen a few people make their transition. Some had favorable results and some had results that were not so favorable. Others' results did not persuade me either way. I continually felt that I was not capable to stop worrying about what other people thought. Hell, even after being with Wild Child, and being so comfortable with him, I still kept Lauren buried. Thus, for years, in the back of my mind, I did not stop thinking about being her.

I did not realize at the time, but all my worry was having a physiological effect on me. The stress was affecting my health. I recall plenty of nights waking up in a cold sweat and laying on my bunk feeling bad because I was faking. I was not who I was meant to be. At that time, Wild Child was gone. I no longer had anyone to confide in, even though I was hanging around the gay guys and transgenders. The gays and transgenders all looked at me like I was just a piece of meat or what they call "trade," which is a manly man.

I began to dress in thongs and booty shorts secretly. When my cellmate, whoever he was, went outside or was asleep, I would put on those clothes and feel as sexy as hell. I had many urges to explore my femininity yet few ways to do so. Granting Lauren, a bit of freedom to dress and express felt liberating and eased some of my stresses.

I would hide the clothing inside of my property and keep it for a while, but then cold sweats would wake me for a different reason. The fear that officers would search my cell and find my thongs and booty shorts would drive me to discard the clothes that granted me feminine expression. Once the clothes were gone, I would feel relief at the assurance that I would not get caught. Nonetheless, in time, the urge to feel sexy and free would overwhelm my caution and I would make new clothing.

✖ ✖ ✖

I would like to emphasize here that I cannot say exactly when my feminine impulses and urges began. When I was on the streets, none of the homies ever said that I acted feminine in any manner. They never even joked like that, so the birth of my female self is hard for me to pinpoint.

As I think about it, I do recall opening up to my stepdad about my internal conflict and he said that what I told him did not surprise him because when I was a baby, I had some feminine ways. He agreed with me, to an extent, that I was a "mama's boy." Mama's boy being a phrase he encapsulated with hand-signed quotation marks. He said that I used to switch, accentuate my hip swing, when I walked. He also said that there were times when he would catch me walking around limp-wristed, as a princess will do for the lips of a loyal subject. I did not recall these behaviors. I contradicted my stepdad's statements with my own belief that I was hard. He quickly told me that I did not display toughness until my teenage years when I started running around in the streets.

32

LAUREN UNCAGED

I t took me until age 30 to build up enough courage to finally allow Lauren to be uncaged, and for me to be who I am. In a way, I feel like all of the suppression stunted my growth as Lauren. For so many years my feminine side never got the chance to blossom.

At the time, I was housed at the level four Tehachapi State Prison. I was in the Security Housing Unit (SHU) for a conspiracy drug case. The SHU is a cell that is isolated from the general population with next to zero amenities permitted. I was supposed to have six months in the SHU but ended up doing nine. I had quite a lot of time to think.

During this time, I only received mail from my younger sister. No one else bothered to write. I felt alone and rejected. I felt as if no one in the world cared about me. I was depressed and angry. For most of that time, I was miserable. I was unhappy with my circumstances and my life as a whole. I did a lot of reflecting and soul searching. I spent my whole life being and acting like someone that I felt and knew was not me. All of it was out of the fear of being rejected by my friends and the fear of losing the love of my family, mainly my dad.

Every day at an appointed time the correctional staff delivered mail. I would wait for the call of my name and a letter from my family slipped under my cell door. It never happened. I was always distraught. I started asking myself why I should care about what my family and so-called friends thought of me when they were not even here for me or gave a damn about my suffering. All of my friends had stopped writing to me and answering the phone when I called. With all of these thoughts taking laps around my mind, I began to think about how changing into Lauren would affect my kids. That was a burdensome weight on me. I love my children and would never want to do anything to hurt them yet, I was the one hurting on the inside. My thoughts then turned inwardly. I thought about how happy I was when I did hang around the transgenders on the yard. I knew in my soul that Lauren was both tired and fed up with being hidden. She was in pain and was begging to be free.

I have always been close to my sister, even before I came to prison, and I knew that I could tell her anything. Knowing this gave me a form of relief. I did not want to be in prison doing life and not have a single soul in my corner. I told myself that if one person in my family would love me unconditionally, no matter who I am or what I looked like, then I would take a leap of faith and go through with my transition.

I took my time and wrote a three-page letter to my sister stating all my fears, doubts, and hopes. I told her about my unhappiness in the SHU. I wrote candidly about my contemplation to transition to a transgender woman. I shared the things that I had tried sexually and how I envisioned my life. I opened up completely. I held back nothing. The letter of love and acceptance I received from her in return offered tremendous support. It brought tears to my eyes. It brought me the courage I needed to move forward.

During this time, I questioned my sexual attraction to women. I knew that for my entire life I had been attracted to women; not because that was what the Bible taught, or because that is what I was told I should do, but because everything about them turned me on. Their curves, their walk, hell even their smell, is attractive. I loved the whole female persona. It is all sexy. I realized, however, that I had more than just a lust for them. It was more like I envied them. It was also because I was jealous of them and I wanted to be one of them. I loved the way they seemed always to receive attention. I loved everything for which a woman stood. Strength, sensuality, passion, desire, and mystery are all bound inside a woman.

Foremost, I love women's strength. Most people think that men represent strength, but when you look at it, women do. Women are the ones that have the babies and endure all of the pain and stress that comes along with having children. Women are the ones that hold families together, even if and when the men leave. Plus, what is stronger than a woman who can show the emotions of love, compassion, and kindness and then turn an about-face and be fierce and aggressive. Most men show few if any emotions or emotional character, let alone a multitude of subsequent and varying emotions. So yes, women are stronger.

My sister told me of how shocked she was to read my story and how she had cried while writing me back. She said that she had always viewed me as a lady's man and not as some man's lady. At the same time, she expressed her gladness for me that I was searching for myself and my happiness.

In my letter, I explained to her that I was scared that no one would love me if I became a transgender. Her exact response was, "You have been unhappy for years now. You have always worried about what others thought of you. Now it is time for you to worry about yourself. It is time for you to make you happy. I know you have kids and a wife, but in the end, it is about what you feel." She went on to say, "We all love you but if someone in the family does not accept you, then oh well. That means that they did not love you in the first place. Just know that no matter what, I am here for you. Whatever you need, I got you. And, I know for a fact that if mama were still alive, she would still love you just the same."

Reading those words from my little sister, (she was 27 years old at the time), gave me the mental strength to move forward. I decided not to let anything stop me from going through with my transition. I knew that no matter what I felt or who I became, my little sister loved me unconditionally.

Upon my release from the SHU, I found out about my wife's live-in boyfriend. I then understood why I had not heard from her for so long. I tried to push Lauren back into her internal cage, but the information about my wife was the straw that broke the camel's back.

33

HORMONES

I ended up going to the prison psychiatrist. We talked for two hours. I told her about my feelings of being born in the wrong body as well as my fears. When I told her that I was tired of acting like a man just because society said I had to because I was born with male genitals, I knew that I was releasing my pain. I also expressed my exhaustion from living in fear of losing my father's love. I told her that even though I acted like a man, I have always felt as if I were a woman. For my entire life, I have felt this way. I was hurting because I could not freely express myself.

Eventually, the psychiatrist asked me on a scale of one to ten, just how bad was I hurting. Her entire facial expression softened as she noticed the tears pouring down my face as I replied that my pain was an eight. She then explained that I was suffering from Gender Dysphoria (GD.) The psychiatrist scheduled me to stand before a committee of five women that would determine if I should receive hormonal therapy. She made me feel so comfortable as she explained to me that the women were not there to judge me.

At the committee, I did as the psychiatrist explained and told the advisors precisely what I had shared in my psychiatric session. These women listened to me for about an hour. They gave me words of encouragement. They assured me that I no longer had to pretend to be someone that I was not. I no longer had to act like a man.

At the end of the meeting, they unanimously agreed that I was indeed suffering from Gender Dysphoria. They all voted to grant my hormone treatment. As I walked out of the meeting, one of the women stopped me and said, "Welcome to womanhood." Her words lifted a weight off of my shoulders. Relief flooded my spirit. I have never felt happier in my life. Lauren was born and finally free. I no longer had to pretend.

✖ ✖ ✖

I guess all those years of hiding Lauren made my transition even smoother because feminine ways came naturally to me. I did not try to act like a woman. I just acted as myself in every way. It is crazy because I never consciously thought about if I was or was not acting feminine.

The first time I noticed and realized a change in demeanor, was when I got on hormones. I transferred to a prison that has unique and dedicated transgender services. I felt an honest sense of relief knowing that I no longer had to walk around a yard pretending to be hard with an angry look on my face. I was free to let go.

It usually takes a couple of months to a year to see any changes from the hormones. I was still hard bodied like a guy from all of the years of working out. My muscles were still showing. I was sitting at the table with one of my friends. She was an older transgender with whom I would talk. As she spoke, it was as if she was predicting the future. She told me that my face was already looking feminine and how in time, the hormones would start to soften my body. She said that the good thing about me just starting out on hormones was that I was already displaying feminine mannerism and since such mannerisms came naturally to me, I would have no problems with my transition. She said that the hormones would enhance me.

As we spoke, whenever I did something feminine, she would point it out to me, and as she did so, I began to notice my femininity. I indeed started to feel more womanly. Slowly but surely, those who were around me at the beginning stages began telling me how different I looked and how much for the better my body was adapting and changing.

Soon, other transgender girls started asking me how long I had been on hormonal treatment. My breasts were growing and filling in at a rapid pace.

The bigger they grew, the more people took notice and complimented me. I guess I was lucky that my body developed rapidly because some girls do not see any significant results for years. My breast became full in less than six months. I thought I would have large breasts because both my mother and grandmother had big breasts. Plus, on top of that, most of the women on both sides of my family have large breasts. They are all in the C and D cup range.

Not too much longer, I began to notice the breakdown of my muscular structure. My body took on the curves of a woman; there was a softening of my skin; my hair grew longer faster; my features became more petite; my cheekbones started to stand out. It was not a surprise to me when every morning as I looked into the mirror, I started seeing my mother's face.

All of these changes happened within my first year on hormones. When I returned to the doctor, she raised the hormone dosage because my testosterone levels were still high. Plus, my doctor felt that a higher dosage would allow me to develop even further. Indeed it did! I seriously began feeling the effects of the hormone increase on my body. My breasts got even more prominent. I had dramatic mood swings. I was hormonal all of the time. I would cry even when I was happy. I would get snappy, even angry, and then become overjoyed all within a matter of minutes. I started growing more emotionally attached to my lover. I also noticed my mental state change. I felt more sensitive toward things and situations than I normally, or should I say, the older version of me, would feel. Finally, I became more bitchy (LOL.) I might find myself quarreling with my lover for some small thing like not acknowledging me fast enough when I called his name. Or, I might call him out because he left the cell door open or even closed it when I wanted to go out.

I did not notice my sudden weight gain until I had put on almost fifty pounds. I knew that my breasts, thighs, and butt growing played a part in those fifty, but I also gained weight in my stomach area. Upon initiating hormones, I had no idea that I would have all sorts of weird food cravings. I was always hungry. I began to worry about my eating so I opened up and talked to other transgenders and my doctor so that I could have a better understanding of exactly what my body was experiencing. I also wanted to learn about what was yet to come.

I learned that my symptoms were not outrageous nor were they abnormal. I was having the symptoms of a pregnant woman. My body was equating the high dosage of estradiol and spironolactone as if I were having a baby. Like any cis-gendered woman that is pregnant, I started experiencing pregnancy cravings and weight gain.

Now I can catch myself and acknowledge when I am becoming hormonal. I am far better at controlling it. I can feel the symptoms.

Regardless of everything said thus far, with hormones there are more upsides than down. There are many days when I am high off life and feeling good. There are many times when my body naturally glows from the moment I open my eyes until the moment I go back to sleep. On these days, everyone seems to notice me and comment. Their words and my elated feelings bring out the true woman in me. We call it "feeling our fish." I love to feel my womanhood grow.

34

BISEXUAL & TRANS

Some people think that it is strange for me to be transgender and, at the same time, be attracted to cis-gendered women. I don't. Even though I had been with men and was also in a relationship with one, I was not automatically attracted to men. It is hard for me to say why I felt this way. Most of the guys that I have been with started off as friend–ships, then the chemistry built. That is how I was able to develop feelings for them. I guess it is safe to say that I am a bi-sexual transgender.

A few years into my transition, I noticed that I started looking at men in the same way that any woman who is not a lesbian does. Honestly, that shocked the hell out of me. I am not sure if the years of being on hormones are what cause me to look at men like they are some delicious pork chops or T-bone steaks but whatever the reason is, I do. Or, maybe it happened when I finally was able to shake the negative information I was fed while growing up about two guys being together. All I know for sure is that I have found myself. All that the bible says and all that people believe can no longer be my guide in this life. I have accepted myself for who I am, and I realize I have to live for myself, not because of forced beliefs. I have the power to discard what others may want me to do or to be. All that being said, while I am attracted to women, this electric feeling compelling me to look and lust at men is for me (LOL.)

35

LAWRENCE VS LAUREN

A s Lauren, I have been asked a lot of questions, some questions I find crazy, like if I was "turned out." Being turned out means to be unwillingly forced to do sexual acts, and, later on, choose to do those same sexual acts. Or you may have been manipulated into doing sexual acts and then later decide to participate in those same acts.

No, I have not been turned out. I was never touched or forced to do things sexually. My thoughts and feelings came out on their own. Of course, I have heard of people who suffered sexual abuse and the abuse twisted their sexual life, but in my life that never occurred. I am also keenly aware that quite a few people who are gay or transgender fall victim to someone else's predatory ways. That has never been, nor ever will be the case with me.

My transition gave me the same feelings I had when my children were born. I had all of those proud feelings that a parent gets when there is a new life brought in to this world. The only difference this time was that instead of a child being born, it was me; it was Lauren.

Lauren can express herself in ways that Lawrence could never have dreamed. One of the reasons for this is because I have been blessed to experience the thoughts and feelings of being both a man and a woman. My thoughts as Lawrence were utterly different than those of Lauren. They are on opposite ends of the spectrum. Our views on life are drastically opposed as well.

As I take the time to dwell on this, I realize that Lawrence's thoughts were not even his own. He based his views on what he was told. He was a follower who convinced himself that he was a leader and being a man. Lawrence convinced himself that everything he believed was right because others were there to confirm his truths.

Lauren, on the other hand, is an authentic independent thinker. She sees life differently. Lauren is open and free. She knows that just because something is told or even taught to you, doesn't mean that it is the truth or even right. Lauren thinks outside of the box. She judges for herself. She looks past the social stereotypes and dogmas.

Lauren knows that not every problem has to be solved in the man's way of aggression and anger. Difficulties do not have to result in a contest of pride. A problem can be solved with the touch that is unique to a woman. Problems can be smoothed. Problems can be solved with finesse.

Lauren can see the beauty in everything and everyone. She is capable of respecting other's thoughts and feelings. She accepts people for who they are. As I think back on when I first began this journey, I recall worrying if people that I loved would view me as some science experiment gone wrong (LOL.) But, in the end, I knew that I could not let worry get the best of me. I had fought far too hard and endured too many stressful nights to turn back. I finally womaned up and began telling each of my family members of my change. I had already spoken by letter to my sister, so I then went on to tell my two brothers.

36

TELLING MY FAMILY

I started with my older brother. After all, he had been in my life since the day I was born. Needless to say, I was worried, but he was instantly happy for me. He understood and said, "No matter what, I love you, sis." And, whenever I speak with him, there is no change in the level of respect and love he has for me. He is always saying, "sis this," and "sis that."

Now my little brother was happy for me as well, yet he was honest in saying that he was a bit leery of gay people. He told me that he respected the LGBT community. He said that he a few situations where gay guys tried to hit on him and that he was made uncomfortable by the guys that tried to hit on him. As we talked, I mentioned how I feared that he would be disappointed with me. Like my big brother, he explained that we are family and that he would never stop loving me because of who I am. To this day, he has not changed towards me. Nevertheless, I can tell that it is hard for him to accept that his big brother is now his big sister.

My brothers were a smaller worry for me than telling my dad and stepdad. My brothers were grateful that they had heard about my change from me instead of hearing it from someone else. I was scared as hell to tell my dad and stepdad. After all, they were the two most powerful male figures in my life and both of them had expressed homophobia as I grew up. I wrote to both of them.

My stepdad swiftly replied. He wrote that my mom had changed his outlook on life and the way that he thought about things. He said that he realized that everyone needs love. He told me that he loved me even if he does not agree with my life change. His words stuck with me because he said that he knew that my prison sentence carried a lot of time and he was happy for me. He realized that I am now able to find myself and my happiness even in such a depressing place like prison.

My biological dad took about two months to respond to my letter. Honestly, I did not know what to expect because he was the reason, as I have mentioned several times, for Lauren hiding for thirty years. In his letter, my dad said he did not recall saying homophobic words to me. He said he was sorry if he had. He went on to say that no matter what, I was his child and that he would always love me. He said that he wished I would have told him years ago about my struggles. His words were music to my spirit. They were nourishment to my starving soul. After telling him and receiving his acceptance, I indeed started feeling comfortable with myself. I had an inner peace, but it was not complete. I had not lost any of my family, yet I still had three more important people I needed to tell. I had to tell my wife and my two children.

Before I did, I spoke to some of my uncles and aunts and even a few of my cousins. In a way, I guess I was delaying the inevitable. Thanks to my dad, they had already heard about my change. They were more curious about how long I had hidden this. They all wanted to know why I had taken so long. Amazingly, the more family members I told, the easier it got and the more comfortable I became. Even still, I dreaded telling my wife and kids. Losing them would have been devastating.

I learned that not speaking with my wife was my biggest mistake. She felt that no one should have mattered before her. She felt that everyone else knew and it hurt her because all of our business was in the mouths of others before she had the chance to speak with me and see if we could work things out.

My wife told me that her hurt did not come from the fact that I had hidden who I am from her for our whole lives; nor did her hurt come from the fact that I had gotten on hormones and changed entirely from the person that she knew; no, her hurt was because I had not told her first. She said that she felt used and betrayed.

Even still, in spite of all of her hurt, and even in the midst of her confusion over who I am, she accepted me with open arms.

My children were already teenagers and had their views on life. My news to them was not shocking or wrong. They assured me that they loved me all the same. Nonetheless, I felt that it bothered them a little.

When my family came to visit me, I offered a full understanding of who I am. Being able to talk with them all face to face was refreshing. They told me that I looked just like my mom and that they would get used to the change in me. Both of my children said that the only thing that was tripping them out was the fact that I had breasts that were bigger than their mother's.

I can say that after our visit, I finally became 100% comfortable with myself. I had no more worries and burdens to carry. The people who truly mattered to me in my life loved me unconditionally. I now know for a fact that I have let all of my hang-ups go.

37

I AM EVERY WOMAN

Since my transition, I have had a few people ask who Lauren is. Who is the woman? I then begin describing myself as a person. I describe my characteristics and the aspects of myself that stand out. I describe my personality. Then the person will re-word the question and say something like, "No, no, no. What type of woman are you?" I ask this person what exactly she means. Then I am asked if I want to get the sexual reassignment surgery (SRS). I am asked if I want to get all of the curves like the transgenders in Hollywood or on T.V. I am asked if I am the type of woman who wears make-up all of the time.

My answer to all the above is, no. I am not a showy type of person. Nor, am I the type of woman to feel as if I need to do all of those surgeries to my body so that I can look perfect or better or how society deems what is perfect. I marched to society's drum beat before as Lawrence. Lauren will never make that mistake.

Unbeknownst to the people that ask these questions, I needed to stop and think about Lauren's character? When I describe myself in response, I realize that I am not answering the real intent of their questions, although I am telling them what they truly need to know.

First off, I am not a type of person, I am me; I am Lauren. No surgery, make-up, hairstyle, tight clothes, or anything like that defines me as a woman. Nor should those things be considered the summation of any woman. Those things are merely ornaments and decorations for this body.

Lauren is a respectable, loving, kind, compassionate, sympathetic, and empathetic person who never turns down someone in need. She is very loyal, even to a fault. Lauren is an intelligent, strong, and beautiful black woman. She can be sweet and innocent, then in the blink of an eye, she can be stern and have an, "I don't play that" attitude. Lauren is an athlete. Some even call her a tomboy, especially when she is on the basketball court. Depending on her mood, Lauren can then turn right around and be sexy, seductive, and feminine. Lauren is business minded and a focused person. Lauren has visions and goals she is striving to achieve every minute of every day. Her aspirations exceed her current circumstance and situation. Lauren is a hustler and a go-getter. Lauren is as the song sings:

"I'm every woman. It's all in me."

I guess I can go on and on about who I am and the qualities that I possess. In truth, there is no way to box all women into a type because each of us is different. We all have our characteristics. We are all unique. The inner being is what defines you. No magic phrase can truly encapsulate what makes me a woman. Even still, if I had to use one word to describe Lauren, a word to describe me but not define me, I would use the word "chameleon." My mood and demeanor are subject to change, but the true essence of who Lauren is, never will.

38

WE ARE ALL GOD'S CHILDREN

Now I have also been asked a few times if I regret any part of my transition. I can honestly say, no! I am pleased with who I am. There is nothing about it that I regret. I supposed I should restate that and say the only thing I regret is that I did not make this change sooner in life. I regret hiding. I would have enjoyed knowing this happiness far sooner. Had I made this transition sooner, I would have experienced more of life through Lauren's eyes. Her growth would not have been stunted. I also believe that had Lauren been flourishing out on the streets, the situation that has me in prison would have never occurred. More importantly, I never would have struggled and would have saved myself a lot of pain.

I am not saying that having to hide my identity played a part in my criminal attitude. Not at all. I did those crimes because of the choices that I made. Yes, I did a lot of my crimes out of peer pressure because the people I grew up around were doing illegal things and I did not want them to think that I was a square or that I was not down with them. I did not want them to say that I was not with it.

I believe that it is important to get as many people as possible to read my story and get to know me as a person. Because, although there are thousands, and maybe even millions of transgenders in this world, and although some of our stories may sound similar, we each have different stories to tell. We are all unique. Also, I hope that by reading this someone's eyes will be opened with the realization that transgenders are not to be judged and cast out. We are just like everyone else. We are God's children.

MOUTHPIECE

PIMPING & PANDERING • HUMAN
TRAFFICKING • CONSPIRACY TO KIDNAP

1

DISCLAIMER

A s this story is being told, I wish to convey that there are some things I am not at liberty to disclose. See, I have an active case and a lot of things I have done in my past are still being investigated. With my case under investigation, I can still be arrested and tried and receive more prison time if pertinent details are revealed in this book. I am not a snitch and I am not here in prison for snitching.

I am not trying to be vague either; it is just that this is the reality of how things are. If you were raised in the streets, then you know where I am coming from. If you are not from the streets then it means that I am not trying to put anyone else in this God forsaken, damn place. Prison will strip you of your heart, soul, and pride if you allow it.

A prison veteran once told me this, "They can cage your body but they can never lock up your mind."

I have chosen to reveal as much as I am both comfortable with and willing to without compromising my morals, principles, and without implicating anyone else.

2

P.I.M.P

Pimping comes as natural to me as swimming does to a fish, or as soaring comes to an eagle. I am raw and uncut, yet I make absolutely no apologies for it. Abrasiveness is my texture; smoothness is my style. With a sense of me now being felt, I am willing to allow you a larger glimpse into who I am, the world in which I operated, and, in the process, share with you what true pimping is.

In truth, I know that there are a precious few people capable of handling a full view of who I am. Not many of you who read these words will either be willing or objective enough to absorb the realities of the world in which I thrived and flourished.

Pimping means many things to many people. When the majority in society hear the term, they instantly visualize some dude dressed in a cheap ass suit, probably looking like a clown, with a Fedora on. They may think of a guy standing on the street corner with a toothpick sticking out of his mouth and a fur coat on, barking orders to a group of scantily clad, confused, and scared women.

In the real world, pimping is nothing like that.

The acronym P.I.M.P. stands for a variety of things. Here are a few: Power In My Palm, Professional In Manipulating People, Pussy In My Palm, and others. For me P.I.M.P. simply means, Paper In My Pockets.

Money truly does make the world go around. It sets the stage for everything from social class to the perception others have of you. Not that I give a damn about how other people see me or even accept me. Money also opens doors for you that are normally closed. See, there is one truth that is universal; if you don't have money, then you cannot acquire the finer things in life. You cannot sustain yourself. These are lessons I learned at an early age.

3
_____

MENTORS

I was born at Brookside Hospital in San Pablo, California. I lived
with my mother. I am her first born child. I have a younger sister
and brother with whom I get along with very well. We are all close as
a family. Even still, I have not always lived with them.

I define myself as a grandma's boy, meaning I spent a majority of my
time with my grandmother. She spoils me to no end, and even now, I
know that there is nothing she wouldn't do for me. She has always
been my rock. Her love is unconditional and unwavering. No matter
where I am, or what I do, I know that my grandma's love is there
for me.

Now even though I am a real street person, a product of the rawness
in which I lived, I was raised in the church. I had to attend. There
was no question about it. Both my mother and grandmother were
exceptionally great parents.

Yet, I would not or could not say the same about my sorry ass father.
Although I knew where he lived and could have gone to see him or

spent time with him whenever I desired, I had no desire whatsoever to do so.

I believe his absence in my life made me a better person. It made me a stronger man. I learned never to depend on anyone for anything. I am self-sufficient. I am a survivor. I am independent. I do not believe in asking for help. If I need it, I go get it. If I cannot get it, and get it for myself, then I do not need it.

Nor do I seek the approval of other people. I could care less what anyone else says or thinks of me. Why should I? I am a grown ass man and not some wide-eyed, wet behind the ears little boy. See a man does what the hell he wants to do and a boy does what he is told to do.

I do not seek out the praises of other people, nor do I spend my time focusing on those who expend their energies hating on me. Again, I ask, why should I?

✖ ✖ ✖

My family lived in Richmond, California until I was three years old; then my mom packed us all up and moved us to Pinole, California. She eventually ended up marrying my sibling's father.

Even at a young age, there was no secret that I didn't want to live with them, so I ended up moving back and forth between their house and Richmond, where I lived with my grandmother. As I mentioned before, my grandma spoiled me and I learned to take full advantage of that. In spite of her spoiling, she had one rule: she said, "If you are going to live in my house, you are going to go to church."

There is no doubt in my mind that my grandma is the one who taught me how to be a man. She did not sugar coat anything. She worked as a school teacher for twelve years. I used that to my advantage. When

I did not want to be in my own class, I would throw a nutty (act out) and my teacher would, to calm me, send me to my grandma's class. I still was not allowed to just sit around. I would do the work her classroom was assigned. My grandma taught me to work for what I wanted and to be a go-getter.

She eventually switched careers and became a lunch lady. I saw that no matter what, she was a hustler in the sense that she took care of her business. She eventually retired.

Now let me state, I had a relatively smooth upbringing, even before my mother gave birth to my siblings yet we still started struggling and ended up on welfare, receiving food stamps and living in section eight housing. Eventually, things grew bad between my mother and her husband and he ended up leaving her with three kids to care for on her own.

As I think on this, I can say that both my mother and grandmother were prime examples for me of what a loyal woman, a true woman, a dedicated woman, is. They are sparkling examples of the definition of a woman with values and morals. They taught me that for a woman to value a man, that woman must value herself first and foremost.

If a woman does not respect herself, if she disregards her own appearance and wellbeing, then you cannot expect for her to do those things to or for you. So, there is no doubt that my grandma and my mother's teachings, even when they had no idea that they were doing so, were the catalyst for my views on life.

Likewise, seeing my mom's struggles shaped my personality. Her struggles solidified my views of the world. It is about taking care of myself and my family by any means necessary. See, it is clear cut, you are either with me or against me. And, if you are not with me, then I am going to make it my business to roll right over you. So, if you are on the opposite side of me then it is in your best interest to get the hell out of my way.

I also believe that if you are down for me, then I will be down for you. I help those who help me. If you push me, then I will pull you and vice versa. If you are loyal to me, then I am, without a doubt, loyal to you. When you are living a street life, that is just how it has to be. If not, then others are going to walk all over you.

✖ ✖ ✖

W hen it comes to my dad, well, I really do not have much to say about that nigger except fuck him! I feel this way because he knew who I was and where I was, but he never lifted a finger to help me. Nor did he make any type of effort to be in my life. As a man, and as a father, he should have fought harder for me, the way I do to remain in my own children's lives. Honestly, what does it say about him as a man if he will not even fight for his own flesh and blood?

Yet in spite of this, I can say that I did learn a couple of things from his sorry ass. For one, I learned how to be man enough not to run from my responsibilities, like he did. After all, running away does not stop the responsibilities from being there. Also, I learned in part, how to get my hustle on. I learned to drive hard to get what I want. See, the one thing my father did was, he didn't let anything stand in his way or stop him, not even his kids. He is the true definition of a go-getter. In a way, he taught me just like my grandma did, but in a different way.

✖ ✖ ✖

I moved to Texas when I was about nine years old and I stayed for a year. I went there with my mom and her boyfriend. It was too much for me in the sense that even at that young of an age, I missed the streets of Richmond, so I returned. Texas just wasn't for me. I knew I needed to be in the middle of the action. I needed to be where things were happening.

✖ ✖ ✖

T he main influence in my life was my uncle. Although my drive and hustle came from my dad and grandma, my uncle was the main force in shaping my attitude. He was in the streets and did everything the streets offered. He was, by far, the truest definition of a hustler. By that, I mean that any and everything that crossed his hands, he sold. Drugs, CD's, DVD's, anything, he pushed. Hell, he was even a stripper. His stripping names were "Mello Mel" and "Taste of Chocolate."

He was also a pimp in the truest sense of the word. Yes, he sent hoes to go and get his paper, but he also carried guns and was a force to be reckoned with. I watched on many occasions as he both talked his way into and out of shit all the time. I have even seen him driving a cab at one point just to get his paper.

Once, he rode me around in his car and gave me a gun. He pointed to someone walking down the streets and said, "Okay, you want to be with this street life shit? Well go out there and get with it and come back with everything in that nigger's pockets." Needless to say, I did just that and it was an exciting feeling and an experience I will never forget.

✖ ✖ ✖

I realized at an early age that I wasn't good at stealing, unlike many of my friends. I remember once when my grandma, my mother, and I, went to a store. While they were preoccupied, I stole a black and brown toy cap gun. I managed to walk out of the store and got away with it. Excited about my accomplishment, I showed it to my mother, who was none too pleased. She, in turn, showed it to my grandmother. My grandmother took me back to the store and made me give the gun back.

Somehow, I found myself in front of a police officer. He sat me down and talked to me. I don't remember everything he said, but I do remember him asking me what I had learned from the situation: "I learned that I do not like my grandma or the police," I said.

I also remember my mother telling me that she would not have told on me but that the gun looked too real. I never thought that that was a good enough reason.

4

_____

STREET ETHICS

There is no one defining moment, one crystal clear point of reference that I can pinpoint and say, "Ah-ha, that is the time when I first learned about crime." Crime has always been an intricate part of my life. It has always had a prevalent presence in the environment in which I grew up.

It was nothing out of the ordinary for me to see someone selling drugs, smoking weed, getting high, or being robbed on a regular basis. Many of the people doing the selling, smoking, and robbing were people I knew and hung out with.

Stealing was as commonplace as breathing. No one really gave much ethical thought to the fact that we were stealing. It was just something that we did. Most of the time, it was to survive. Some people stole to have food to eat. Some did it to have nice clothes to wear and sometimes people stole just because whatever it was that they were stealing, was there.

The fact that my mother was not able to give me the things I wanted was definitely a contributing factor in my criminal ventures. Wanting to keep pace with all of the things my friends seemed to have, gave me the motivation I needed to go out and get it at any cost. I was definitely trying to keep up with the "Joneses." I knew that the streets held what I needed and I knew that the only way I could lay my hands on it was by getting in the streets and taking it.

✖ ✖ ✖

L ike stealing and other crimes, violence, in almost every sense of the word, has been a significant part of my life. Everything from fighting to seeing someone get popped (shot) and lose his life, has been common. I have seen dudes beat their women and I have seen dudes getting beat down by other dudes. I have seen groups of girls take off on a single girl just because they hated that she looked better or that she was more popular. Hell, I have had to handle my own business on many occasions. I have had to bust (shoot) on some dudes as well.

I was probably around ten years old when I got into a fight with someone because I was protecting my cousin. See, this Mexican guy was bagging (making jokes) on my cousin and my cousin couldn't take it. My mom, she's a real thug, told me, "Go outside and beat his ass baby." I knew I had to do it or suffer the consequences and get my own ass whipped. I knew my mom wasn't making idle threats. So, I did exactly that, I went outside and beat the hell out of the dude.

5

ANGER MANAGEMENT

One thing that is an asset for me is that I have never been the type of person to let my temper rule me. I rule over it. I can be furious with someone, even to the point of wanting to kill that person, but he would never know because I will keep my anger under wraps.

I will admit that there has been a time or two when I did succumb and let anger get the best of me. Most times I will think rationally and play things out in my head. I will examine the wide variety of options to a situation and decide which would be the best course of action. Then, there are times that I won't. I will just let myself go. I will simply react. I will allow myself to give in to the rage that floods me and let my anger run its course.

Being from where I am from, Richmond, California, you have to be like this. It is a way of life. Sometimes words are not enough. Sometimes, words just don't get through to people. Sometimes, they only understand one language: they only understand the language of violence.

There were times when I would be all gung-ho. I would be like, fuck it, and say let's just go all out. I would feel like there was no need for talking. I would only desire to get things started. To be engrossed in violence.

For the most part, and as an adult, I realize that I now have far too much to lose. Plus, I know that time thinking is time well spent. Yes, there are times when you have to just do what you have to do to survive, and times when you have to just not give a damn to survive. You have to live life. The best bet is to plan things out and execute them in a way so you assure yourself the best of outcomes.

6

UNREQUITED LOVE

The first time I can say that I ever truly had my heart broken was also the last time that I allowed myself to be gullible and be in that situation. It was the last time I got my heart broken.

I was around thirteen and was infatuated with this girl, I mean I really liked her. I was all in. Unfortunately, many young men are vulnerable at that age, and some even carry this type of mindset into their adult years.

Still, it was clear that she never felt the same way towards me. While I was busy being all caught up and blinded by love, and while I was playing the square role, the hoe was out getting money for some other dude. I was being a real simp. Not only that, I actually walked in and caught her having sex with one of my partners. That alone showed me how scandalous females truly are. They are the sneakicst species on the face of this earth. Thus, I have adopted the motto, "Never trust a bitch!"

Now I keep my heart shut down. I keep it locked away and refuse to allow it exposure to such weak, false feelings. See, before I ever put my all into a woman again, she is going to have to go all out to prove herself worthy of me. She is going to have to show me that she is someone who can contribute to me. She has to show me what she can bring to the table. She is going to have to go above and beyond the call of duty.

Common-sense dictates that all women are not hoes, and I know this. But, I also know that all women have hoe tendencies. I do not think that such tendencies are a bad thing. Most women are just too shy to act on those feelings. It just takes the right man at the right time to bring it out of them. All they need is the right guidance. They need a hand to lead the way.

7

A TURNING POINT

I really started acting out violently when I was fourteen. It was a conscious decision on my part.

Two of my partners and I broke into a house and stole three guns. We each took one. After that, I started thinking I was John Gotti. I felt that way because, before I had my own gun, I used to hold guns for my uncle. Age fourteen marked the first time I shot at someone. It was one of the most euphoric experiences I have ever had. It was a rush like none other.

We were out walking and doing what we did, just hanging out and talking shit to each other, smoking weed and bragging about all the hoes we were having sex with. This was about three days after we had stolen the guns. We noticed a car circling the block. It did this several times. One of my homies said, "If that damn car hits the block one more time, we need to light it up." Sure enough, the car came around the corner once more. Just as it passed by us, all three of us pulled out our guns and let loose. We lit the car up.

✖ ✖ ✖

It wasn't long before I started feeling like the entire world was against me. Everyone started showing their true colors. They were all about them, so I consciously made the shift in my mind to start being all about me. I always put me first. That was one of the best decisions I could have ever made in my life.

8

MOUTHPIECE MAGIC

My teenage years were when my frame of thinking really started to take shape. I was already becoming independent in that I was not living with my mom or anyone. I stayed out and hung out with my homies and basically did me. Meaning, I did whatever in the hell I wanted to with no questions asked.

Thinking back, I was around fourteen when I realized for the first time, that words can either make or break someone. I came to understand that the things I said held a power unlike anything else. With this knowledge, it was not long before I began to see that saying the right thing, to the right person, could get me whatever I wanted in life.

I once watched my uncle talk a female out of her whole check. I thought to myself, "Man, this is amazing." I loved it. I love the way a female can be believing the stuff you are saying. I knew that every word my uncle said to the lady was a lie, but she was hanging on to his every word, as if for dear life. She was going through all sorts of emotional changes. She was completely caught up. It was then that I realized something profound. See, if you can lie good enough to the point that you believe your own lie, then it is easy as hell to get someone else to believe it.

The amazing thing is, this isn't some new concept or an out of the ordinary perception. In fact, it happens every day in every conception of life, all over the world. It happens especially in this country in courthouses during trials.

The prosecutors and defense attorneys do this for a living. They both tell their version of a story, most of what is said by both sides are lies. The one who lies the most convincingly, the one that is most believable, wins over the jury.

Now granted, sometimes the story, the different versions of it, will be sprinkled with a few facts, just to lend credence to the telling, but for the most part, it is all speculation.

✖ ✖ ✖

I was going on fifteen when I officially started living on my own. Up until then, I was basically going back and forth from my mom's to my grandma's, and on occasion, spending a couple of days with one girl or another.

When I started doing shit for myself, I experienced a whole new level of independence. I felt liberated. My mom wanted me home and I wanted to be in the streets. I decided to do things my way and ended up in the streets full time. I was going all out.

I am a self-assured person. I only depend on one person and that is myself. If I make a wrong decision then that is on me. I make no excuses. I view each lesson as God's blessing. I take my own chances and make my own choices.

It is like, a person will jump into the ocean and start swimming, knowing that the water is filled with sharks. Even so, he will still do it. He takes a chance, and in some way, gets an absolute thrill out of it, out of making that choice. That is how I am. I take my own chances.

9

SCHOOL AIN'T SHIT

The last grade I attended in school was either the tenth or eleventh. I am not quite sure. I was, however, what one would consider an overachiever.

In my classes, whenever I chose to go, I had all A's and B's. I knew the work but hated doing any form of homework. I enjoyed clowning around, having fun with my friends and, of course, smoking weed. I loved the attention girls gave me. The fact that I knew I could get anything I wanted out of them by just saying the right things, made the challenge of getting something from them even more satisfying.

A lot of the time, I would just sit around with my partners and just shoot dice and talk shit about people. It was during some of these "clowning" sessions when the truth would really hit you because the things we said were raw and uncut. We would show our asses. If you were dressed like a bum, we would talk shit about you. If your hair was nappy or your breath stank, we would clown you about it. School was nothing more than a fashion show for most of us.

Feelings were never a factor. If you were working with feelings and wanted to get all butt hurt, and if you felt as if you wanted to do something about it, then you would just get your ass kicked.

10

KEEN ON DRUGS

The first time I used any type of drugs, I was around eleven or twelve years old. I had a friend who was bi-racial, half Mexican and half white. He was hella cool, but the crazy thing is, his grandmother was a stone-cold racist.

It was over at his house that I met his sister, who I was trying to have sex with, and she gave me my first taste of weed. She rolled up a blunt and shared it with me. I felt relaxed. I remember thinking that it was the best feeling in the world. I vowed that if I could get past my mother, I would be smoking weed each and every single day. Even now, I love myself some good weed.

I was fourteen when I guess you can say I graduated from weed. I started sipping syrup. Syrup is simply Promethazine and Codeine, or cough syrup. I also started doing prescription pills, mainly Narcos, Vicodins, Percocets, and on a few occasions, a mixture of them together. They are all opioids. I also started doing ecstasy. I had seen other people popping them and finally thought, "Why the hell not?" Ecstasy was an awesome experience. I never graduated from doing it. I just got locked up and can't get my hands on any.

✖ ✖ ✖

W hen it comes to drugs, there are two categories: drugs to be up, hyper, and moving at a million miles a minute and drugs to be down. These drugs are known as downers. They are relaxed, chill, and basically mellowed out. I prefer downers. Ecstasy is an upper. When I am down, I don't get into trouble. I stay mellow. I am cool and kicked back. I am relaxed. It is the same with heroin. The amount you take effects just how mellow you are.

The thing about heroin is, I never actually tried it when I was out on the streets. It was only when I came to prison that I began to indulge. One of the reasons I like downers is because when I am in such a relaxed state, it reminds me of when I was out on the streets. It is an escape for me, and it takes me away from prison.

There are not too many words I can use to describe prison except that is unlike anything on earth. There is nothing but a bunch of tough ass acting dudes, strutting around, acting like they can't be touched by anything or anyone. There is far too much testosterone and not enough relief.

Although many people find their relief in either cards, fighting, or other means, I, on the other hand, find my relief in getting high. I get faded, workout, and talk a gang of shit. I kick it with a few select people, and then, I only do that on occasion.

CAREER PROSPECTS

I was never good at selling dope, although I tried doing it for a few rounds. I remember I got into it with this one female. I was probably around fourteen or fifteen. She gave me five G's (grams) of cocaine but, as I said, I wasn't too good at selling it, so I just did whatever was needed to get it off me. I was selling the stuff dirt cheap. To be totally honest, I was more focused on getting money from her.

FIRST TIME GETTING SHOT

No matter what I chose to do, violence has always been around me. I have been stabbed a few times, by my babies' mothers, and I have been shot twice.

The first time I was shot I was either fifteen or sixteen years old. I was fortunate that the bullet only grazed me on my left hip. At the time, I was half-ass pimping. Thinking that I was the man, basically feeling myself. I also thought I was invincible. There were about six or seven of us just hanging out in front of my great-grandmother's house smoking weed, drinking, and talking shit to each other like we always did. She lived on the south side of Richmond. All of a sudden, a car came around the corner and someone inside started letting off (firing shots at the group of us). We scattered and started running in every direction. I don't know exactly when it happened because I was jumping fences and bending corners as fast as I could. It wasn't until I actually looked down and saw the blood covering the left side of my shirt that it dawned on me that I was shot. That was when it began to hurt.

When I got to my mom's house, I didn't mention being shot. I just put some alcohol on the wound and bandaged it up until the bleeding stopped. I knew that if my mom found out, she would have whipped my ass. Plus, I had no desire to hear her ranting and raving, knowing that it would go on for days.

The amazing thing is, being shot seemed to make me even more popular with women. They catered to me and of course, I ate all the attention up and used it to my advantage.

13

UNCLE KILLED

I was fifteen when one of the hardest and most hurtful things I have ever had to face happened: my uncle was killed in front of me. He was shot by the San Pablo police. He didn't have a gun or any other kind of weapon on him. That was the moment I knew in my heart that I hated the police. They took from me the one person who was like a father.

His death helped turn my heart cold and made me embrace a "fuck the world" attitude. That is the attitude I hold to this day.

14

ROMANCE

I recall going to school and this one girl was really trying to come at me with some negative type of hype saying she was better than me because I was wearing the same outfit that I had worn the day before. Instead of feeling bad about it, I pulled out a wad of cash and flashed it at her. She was stuck. She couldn't do anything but respect that. From then on, the females were all on me.

I was seventeen when I met one of the first women I can say I was captivated by. Her name was Lea. She was living in a section of Richmond, California known as the "Kennedy Manor." She was light skinned with green eyes and had the most perfect set of lips a woman could hope to ever have. I mean this woman really had me stuck.

I loved everything about her. I loved her vibe. She was down to earth, loyal, understanding, and had this quiet confidence. Yet, she allowed me to be me. She wasn't trying to change me in any way.

I still recall the clothes she had on the first time I met her. That is how powerful of an effect she had on me. She was wearing these sexy little shorts. In my mind and heart, I knew that I had to have her. In fact, I wasn't the only one caught up in her aura. Everybody was trying to get at her. All of them were trying to have sex with her, but she was not having it.

Yet, when they all gave up, I pressed on. That was the day that I learned a very valuable lesson. I learned that persistence is the key to life. Whatever you want or want to do, you have to keep at it. You got to keep going. Failure cannot be an option.

Lea eventually left Richmond and went back to Oregon, but came back one month later. When she did, my persistence paid off and she became mine.

✖ ✖ ✖

The thing is, I never really did the girlfriend thing, especially not the high school girls. I tried to talk to them but quickly realized that they just weren't on my level. I even tried to get them to drop out of school and start ho'ing for me, but they wouldn't. Ironically, most of them are now actually ho'ing, but they don't do it for me.

15

LACE YOU UP ON THIS PIMP GAME

One absolute truth is that pimping is a major business. It is like Home Depot, or IBM, or McDonald's. See, Ronald McDonald is not actually at any of the thousands of Mickey D's around the world. He is not the one working all those long, grueling hours. He is not the one doing those tiring double shifts. Nor has he ever done all the back-breaking labor that is required. No, Ronald is never there.

Like any major business or corporation, the grunts, the minions, the slave laborers, are the ones who are on the grind. They are the ones who shoulder the burdens and do all the work. They are the ones who are responsible for bringing in the money. Just like Ronald, it is my duty to get paid off of a hoe's labor.

Now the first time I realized that this pimping game was really for me, I was around sixteen years old. One of my "OG" (original gangster) homies got at me about how I was doing things. He said, "Youngster, you are out here selling dope and taking all these chances, and for what? You are doing all this for some chump change."

He went on. "You got bitches coming up to you, bringing you food and anything else you want. Why not have them getting you your money too?" He went on to lace me about the pimping game.

He said, "It is like this, you got at least fifty who are feeling you. Now let's just say you approach them all about ho'ing for you. Half of them off the top are not going to be with it, or even want to hear what you have to say about it. So, that leaves you with twenty-five who seem as if they are willing to hear you out.

"Out of that twenty-five, fifteen will really take in what you are saying and really hear you, or even vibe with you. Seven or eight of them will actually listen to what you say and take it to heart.

"Now out of these seven or eight, at least three will actually go out and try to get that paper for you. Now of those three, you have to use your mind and pick one to go on the road with you. You make her your down ass bottom bitch. You take off from there and do your thing."

Now I want to say this, a pimp is what the world wants to label him as. I label myself as an entrepreneur. I believe in getting my money by any means necessary. God blessed me with a mouthpiece and the ability to get people to see my point of view. I am able to get people to see me and understand what I am saying.

I have been blessed to be surrounded by women who want to see me come up, women who want to see me flourish. I have been fortunate to have women who want to see me winning. And, not only that, they want to be there with me as I am winning.

See, the reality is, a lot of people in this world talk about love, but when the bills are due, or when there is no food on the table, or no money in your pockets, I'd like to see you pay them bills with love. I would like to see you getting your empty stomach full with a plate of love. I would like to see you fill your pockets with love and spend that instead of money.

Love is just a word that suckas use to justify being weak. Love is something people claim in order to feel good about being all sensitive.

Now you got a lot of these loose ass women out in the world just having sex with numerous dudes for free. They are doing it for nothing. The only thing they are getting is a nutt. Many of these women are contracting STD's and they are carefree about it. They spend more time in the clinic than they do in school, or in church, or even at their jobs if they have one. They are taking more pills and shots trying to get rid of the stuff they are catching than a pharmacy can supply.

If you are laying up with just one man I can commend you for that. If you are holding him down and doing the monogamous thing, then that's cool. Hell, even if you are the type of woman who has two men, and you are doing your thing with them, I can even respect that. After all, sometimes a person needs one or two lovers to help sate the appetite.

Then, you have all these women who just go around having sex with multiple men. They are so loose that they can't even keep up with all the men they are laying down with.

The truth is, if you are going to be doing all this screwing with all these men, hell, you might as well get paid for it. After all, why not? Hoes are running around here with major back pain because they are always laying on their backs with their legs cocked open. They are talking in high pitched voices because they are having so much oral sex it is probably shoving their tonsils in their throat.

So, if you are going to be doing all of this extra duty, you may as well start getting paid for it. You might as well benefit from all your hard labor.

✖ ✖ ✖

I have earned my money by being a go-getter. Yes, people label me as a pimp because I get my money out of a hoe's ass, but the truth is, I can't stop a woman from believing in me and my dreams, and wanting to help me get there.

See, a lot of people believe in a lot of things. Some people believe in religion. Some people believe in science. Some people believe in myths. But, I learned at a very young age to get people to believe in me.

I don't see myself in any special way or order. I see myself as a determined person who strives for success. I work hard to win. I push the envelope to the limits with the only goal being, to come out on top.

See, the white man has been winning since the dawn of time. He has most of the power and he wields it to his advantage. Well, I want to win off of him, just like he has been winning off of me and my people all these years. Plus, pimping is a hustle and it is my favorite thing to do. It is fun, exciting, challenging, and cool.

So, then why not hustle and get my money from some good-looking women? Especially, when they are willing to help me get it. Why not come up?

✖ ✖ ✖

I hated selling drugs and the one main reason for that is I hate for weird ass people to come up to me. I am somewhat anti-social, yet at the same time, if I am put into a room filled with women, I will shine as bright as the noonday sun. I will bling like brand new money.

Plus, there is no one method to pimping. It is not as if there is a singular blueprint or course that you have to follow. Plus, I have always been good at talking myself into and out of various situations. With that being a truth, then what is so wrong with me talking myself into some money? If a woman is willing to handle her business for me, then I am going to get my money.

I am sure that everyone has heard the old saying, "A closed mouth don't get fed." The Bible says, "Ask and ye shall receive." So that is what I do. I ask women to go out and handle business for me; they do, and come back with that money and I gratefully receive it.

✖ ✖ ✖

I would not be able to keep an accurate account of all the times someone has come up to me and asked me if pimping is about sex. The answer to that is hell no!

And for the record, it is not about beating down a woman either. Pimping is strictly BUSINESS! It is about getting paid. It is about enjoying the fruits of your labor. It is about being a successful business person.

I use the term fruits of your labor because it is hard work honing the pimp craft. There are a lot of haters in this world. Most of them are gunning for you and trying to keep you down. They hate to see me winning. But, they can't stop me because winning is what I do best. It is in my make-up. It flows through my veins. It is in my blood. I am a winner because I am a real nigga.

Women are beautiful. They have a magnetism about themselves, but very few are really capable of tapping into their inner essence. That is what I do. I connect with their inner-energy and help bring it to the surface. I am like their guide.

FIRST CHILD

I was seventeen when I met my first baby's mother. She is the mother of my son. I met her after I had already met Lea. I met her at a mutual friend's home. In fact, it was my cousin who introduced the two of us to each other.

At the time, I had a different style than I have now. I wore my hair in locks and I even went by a different name. I went by the name Hyphie, which was given to me by my cousin, the cousin that introduced me to my son's mom. He was known as Hyphie as well.

But, I also had the name because it fit me. I was a hyper person. I was all over the place and I was honing my "I-don't-give-a-fuck" attitude. I didn't give a damn about anything or anyone.

I remember how she walked into the house and smiled. She had a charm about her. We chilled and ended up smoking some weed. We connected on a deeper level and our love for each other grew.

A ROBBERY GONE WRONG

N ow even though I was connecting with my baby's mother (BM), I was still out there doing my own thing. I was still committed to thugging.

When I turned eighteen, I went to jail for robbery. I was with three of my partners. I was the oldest and the youngest was sixteen. I had gotten an inside scoop from this chick I knew on a lick (job.) A dude was papered up (carrying a lot of cash on him) and we planned to rob him. I found out the time and place where he was going to be and I got with my boys and set things in motion.

We walked from my aunt's house to the BART (Bay Area Rapid Transit) station, then made our way to the target's house. I noticed that the guy's car was not parked at his house. I decided that the mission was going to be bust and we headed back towards the BART station.

Now out of the whole crew, I was the only one with a weapon. I had a high point .40 caliber handgun. I had no problem with using it if it came down to it.

On the way to the BART station, we saw an older lady walking. One of my partners asked if we should rob her. I didn't think she had any money on her so I wasn't too interested in wasting time on her. In spite of this, my boys went off to rob her. I walked to the corner of the street and turned around to tell them to quit wasting their time and to catch up to me. I noticed that they had already started trying to rob the lady and she was fighting back. In fact, she was actually winning the battle. She was giving them a run for their money so to speak. Eventually, they ran off and ran past me. I took off with them.

I was so angry I could hardly think straight. In fact, I was so mad I actually thought about just shooting them right then and there. Hell, not only did they get their asses whipped by an old lady, she only had one dollar and a credit card on her. My anger boiled over and eventually, we all started to argue.

I had my phone on me and we stopped arguing when it rang. It was one of my old hoes calling to tell me she was about to have a baby and she needed money fast. I snatched the dollar and the credit card from my boy's hand and something told me to look back at where the old lady was. I noticed that she was talking on a phone as well. I immediately took off running again.

The entire time that I was running I was talking on the phone. I raced through the BART station, not really knowing where I was going. The police arrived and ended up chasing me. I was doing everything in my power to shake them, but nothing was working. I was jumping over fences like I was an Olympic high jumper. In fact, I ripped my left hand so badly that it required six stitches. Amazingly, the entire time, I was not even worried about the ripped hand or the blood that was pouring out of the wound. I was too focused on running and worried about my pregnant hoe.

I ran for about an hour, but in the end, it didn't do any good. The police had cornered off the entire block and there was no getting around it. Knowing that there wasn't much of a chance of me getting away, I tossed my gun under a parked car.

After all the running around and so much blood loss, my legs gave out on me. Even still, I wasn't just going to give up. I struggled with a female cop. She suddenly fired my shit up (hit me hard). I hit the ground and ended up scaring up my face.

I was charged with robbery. The victim pointed me out and lied on me saying that I was the one who had actually robbed her. I ended up staying in jail for eight days before I managed to bail out. At court, they labeled me a menace to society. I ended up doing a month on house arrest and was forced to wear an ankle monitor.

18

SECOND CHILD

I was twenty-one when I met my second baby's mother. She is the mother of my first daughter. I met her through my cousin James. He's from a part of Vallejo, California known as "The Crest." It was made famous by the rapper Mac Dre.

James called me one day saying that he wanted us to play basketball. At the time, I had a Lexus Coupe SC 400 and a Dodge Charger. Now although a lot of my homies did this, I never was the type of person to go joy riding in stolen cars. I knew that joy riding was one of the quickest ways to wind up locked behind bars. On this kind of street knowledge, I was laced tight by my uncle. He was like a sensei with all the understanding of the streets he had. For example, I was never one to actually rob anyone. I always let the people I was with actually do the robbing. I would just end up getting half of whatever was taken. I always talked other gullible people into doing the actual crime. I had the gift of gab and knew how to use it to my advantage.

Anyway, I went to pick up my cousin James. When he jumped into the car, I asked him at whose house he was kicking it. He told me that it was his aunt's and that she actually wanted to meet me. He said that she had heard a lot of things about me and needed to see if the things she had heard about me were true.

When I walked into the house, I noticed this skinny, young, sexy woman watching James and me. She and I eventually started talking and that, of course, led to us smoking weed. After some time had passed, I asked James where was his aunt who wanted to meet me. I was shocked when he pointed to the same woman I had been talking and smoking with the entire time.

I knew then and there that I had to have her. I had never had a woman who was so interested in my conversation. I was breathing on her like a brand-new fan. (Breathing means I was really putting my game down. I was handling my business.)

I eventually got around to asking her who she was living with and was pleasantly surprised when she told me that she owned her own home. Needless to say, my interest piqued higher than it had been before. The more we talked, the more I learned. She eventually revealed that there was a guy in her past that she was trying to get away from. I was going to make it my business to see to it that she did.

She was the only woman in my life to ever make me wait three or four months before we had sex. Yet instead of that being a bother to me, it not only made things more interesting; it also gave me a deeper respect for her. I knew that she wasn't like any other woman and I was determined to have her in my life at all times, by any means necessary. So, to assure myself of this, I put a baby in her. Even up to this day, she holds a piece of my heart.

19

SHOT AGAIN

I was around twenty-two when I got shot for the second time. I was out spending time with this female who was basically giving me money. I had worked some things out to where every month, the bank was giving me almost three bands (three thousand dollars.) It wasn't much, just a little chump change I used to buy guns and some syrup to sip.

I asked my mom to take me to a bank branch in Alameda, about twenty miles from Richmond. Now I could have gone to any branch of this particular bank and collected my money, but I am meticulous and only wanted to use the bank branch in Alameda.

Reluctantly, my mom agreed. However, the entire time we were in the car, she was ranting and raving about how I was out in the streets too much and needed to slow down. She was preaching about how I needed to stop doing the stuff I was doing and get my life together.

Needless to say, I had no desire to hear all of her complaining. It got so bad that I just asked her to drop me off at my cousin's house, which of course, she refused to do. In fact, she demanded that I listen to her.

Eventually, it became so overwhelming that I threatened to just jump out of the car at the next light if she did not stop her talk. Finally, she relented and took me to my cousin's. Before she left, I gave her a few dollars which she gladly took from me.

✖ ✖ ✖

A t my cousin's, I immediately started smoking weed as soon as I entered the house. They were already blazing and getting high, yet that was nothing out of the ordinary. Eventually, I got around to asking my cousin to take me to the bank. He was reluctant but relented. His one demand was that I leave my gun at the house. Now leaving my gun was something that I just didn't do, and I normally would have had a fit just because he asked, but I gave in because he said that he would take his gun instead.

We did argue over who would do the driving. He had a two-door Benz and I was dying to get behind the wheel. Of course, with it being his car, he won that argument. So, to relax, I stretched out in the back seat with my head laying on the window. I am not sure how long I laid there because I was high. Now one truth about driving is that whoever is doing the driving is supposed to watch the rearview mirror. The driver is the eyes of the car. He is supposed to be paying the most attention. Obviously, my cousin was not doing that. Suddenly, out of nowhere, something told me to look back. When I did, all I saw was this dude driving his car right beside us pointing a gun directly at me with an "I got yo' ass" smile on his face. Just as I was about to yell out a warning, the guy pulled the trigger and I got hit in the mouth. The bullet went through my lip, then through my teeth and then through my tongue and came out on the opposite side. I was fortunate that I had a mouth full of gold and diamonds.

The guy lit the car up. He shot at us thirty-three times including the one that hit me in the mouth. I later found out that I had been shot with a nine-millimeter. My cousin immediately started shooting back. We got off the freeway and my cousin drove me to the hospital. I didn't have any form of bandages except for my coat so I held that to my face, in an attempt to stop the bleeding. The pain was intense.

Once in the emergency room, I had difficulty telling them what had happened to me, and that I had been shot. Blood was by now, everywhere. The security guard, who was inside the emergency room, finally understood what I was trying to say and ran to locate a doctor. I was placed on a gurney but refused to lay down, in spite of all of their efforts to get me to do so. They had no idea that each time I did, I was choking. The nurse was insistent so I reached into my mouth and took out the bullet and threw it at her.

During the course of all the commotion, I called my baby's mother, who eventually ended up understanding me enough and she called my mother. I was taken and prepped for surgery. The only thing I remember after that was a nurse standing over me and instructing me to count backward from one hundred. I made it to ninety-nine and was out cold.

I woke in a room at John Muir's Hospital. I saw that my mom was in the room. She eventually turned on the news and I found out that there were four shootings in Richmond that night. That was when I realized that the homies loved me for real. All of the shootings were done in retaliation for what had happened to me.

It took about three months before the swelling went down enough for me to be able to open my mouth. I was fortunate in that the bullet did not shatter my jaw, but it did fracture it. Even to this day, it has not completely healed.

20

THIRD CHILD

I met my third baby's mother when I was twenty-three. She is the definition of a computer love. I say this because I met her on Instagram. She was so sexy to me. I had no problem letting her black ass know exactly how I felt.

I was bold and direct with her and asked her if I could have her. I even recall what I said. I said, "I like chocolate. Can I have a piece of you?"

She is extremely dark. She laughed and told me how funny she thought I was. We spent time chatting and eventually I asked for her number. We talked for like three or four days.

Now at the time, I didn't have a car. I wanted to go and buy some weed, so I called her and asked if she had a car. She told me that she did. I then made her a proposition: I told her that if she took me to Sacramento to buy some weed, I not only would smoke with her, but I would feed her and whomever else she brought with her. I also agreed to put gas in her car; I ended up filling the car up.

All the time we were on our way to Sac. we talked and started getting to know each other even better. Well, we ended up smoking some good ass weed and getting high and I eventually asked her to spend the night with me. Of course, we began to have sex. It was during the course of this that I stopped and asked her if she wanted to be with me for the rest of her life. She said yes, so I took off the condom I had on and we continued to have sex. Afterward, I told her that she now belonged to me for the rest of her life.

She had my second daughter while I was incarcerated fighting this case. She held me down all the way until she "frogged the fuck off." For those of you who do not know what that means, it means when someone claims to be loyal, real, and all that bullshit, then leaves you when you need her the most.

✖ ✖ ✖

It is crazy because deep down inside, a part of me always knew that hoes ain't shit. That is why my motto is dog them out before they get the chance to dog you.

See, the hoe got close to me and warmed up my icebox (my heart.) She thawed me out, then threw me back out. Now I got frostbite. But, I am not tripping, because I know that hoes are not loyal nor are they truly about shit.

The crazy thing is, even though I am talking a lot of shit about all of my children's mothers, they are all good to my kids. They take care of their motherly responsibilities. They put my kids before anything else and that is how it should be. Plus, on top of that, they are committed to bringing my kids up here to this God forsaken place to see me whenever they are not on some dumb line of thinking.

As I look back, I can say that some of the happiest moments of my life were having my kids. I was eighteen when I had my first child. He was born in 2008. My second was born when I was twenty-two, in 2012. My third was born when I turned twenty-four in 2014, but, as I mentioned, I was incarcerated.

21

MY CRIME

I am currently in prison for human trafficking, which is some real bullshit. My definition of human trafficking is when you are manhandling a hoe. Human trafficking is when you are throwing a bitch in the trunk of a car or something, with her hands and feet tied up and a gag in her mouth, driving her all over the world and forcing her to have sex with any and everybody who is willing to pay.

Now if a hoe is well aware of what is going on and chooses to participate, if she jumps in the car willingly, then that is not human trafficking. The real issue is when Uncle Sam is not getting a piece of the action; when the government is not getting a cut, then it is considered a crime. But, when Uncle Sam can place his greasy ass palms on the money, then it is all good. Hell, just look at Nevada. It is known as the "hoe state." It is all good and legal to go and get a prostitute, but that is because the government is getting a nice piece of the action.

And, on top of that, everyone knows that the criminal justice system is rigged. That is no big secret. And, it is rigged to keep the minority population down, especially the black man. Race is not just about color. It is also about social status.

Now even with that being said, I do not think that racism was a major factor in my case, but politics definitely was. If you do not have a paid lawyer, then you are just assed out. I know I got played. I was used as a stepping stone.

Now as I mentioned earlier, my case is still active and in the courts, so there are not too many things that I can go into detail about. But I can say, I am in here for pimping and pandering, conspiracy to kidnap, and as I mentioned, human trafficking.

Now what I can say is that they have me in here on some real bull-shit. They have me locked up for pimping a hoe I do not even know. A bitch I never even sent to the grocery store, so I damn sure I never sent her out to go turn a trick. She is a person I met for the first time in my life, and as a result, I am now locked up for the rest of my life!

✖ ✖ ✖

The worst moments for me are each and every moment I am caged like an animal in this place and taken away from society. I am being taken from my duties as a father. It does not take a lifetime to rehabilitate a person. Anyone of reasonable, common sense, can rehabilitate within a five-year span. By keeping a person caged up for life, the system is trying to strip you of your soul. Prison is a money-making business. It is pimping at its finest.

The reality is, nothing is going to change. You have people out in society fighting tooth and nail to free a caged animal, yet would prob-ably never lift a finger to help free a human being.

22

MY LEGACY

Two of my fondest memories are when I cut the umbilical cords on my first two kids. I took care of them and bought them everything they needed or wanted. Even though I am locked up, I still am able to provide for all three of my children. That is something that the system and no one else can ever take from me.

23

EPILOGUE TO MOUTHPIECE

Many of you may wonder a few things about me. You might ask yourself if I have such an attitude, and feel the way I do towards women, why then is it so damn easy for me to get them and to get them to do what I say? Why is it that they come running when I call them?

I am going to reveal to you a secret. The key is to get into their heads. You have to captivate their minds. Now I know some guys think that they have this mastered, and they might on some level, but it goes much deeper.

See, you have to captivate a woman on three levels: you have to seize her mentally, elevate her emotionally, and satisfy her physically.

Mentally, you seize her by the things you say, how you say them, and what images the words you speak create in her mind. They will either draw her to you or push her away from you. A woman's mind is like a rare jewel, you need to polish it so that its brilliance can truly shine.

Emotionally, you have to elevate her. You have to make her feel the things you say. You have to wrap her up in your mouthpiece. She has to feel like everything you say is to be valued like gold.

You need to connect with the wide range of emotions that she will express. You have to convince her that you are there to comfort her. See, one minute she can act blissful as if she is on cloud nine. She will even convince you that she is in heaven. Then, the next minute, she can act resentful. She can make you feel like the wrath of God is coming down upon you. Her emotions are a minefield that you have to know how to navigate through. You make one false move and you will blow everything up.

This is the most delicate side of the entire process. Everybody has heard the saying that there is nothing like a woman scorned. If she feels that you are trying to play her, she will burn you in more ways than you could ever think possible.

Now physically, there really is no one way to explain this instruction. Still, I know that most men have this twisted. They really don't have a clue as to how to conquer a woman and dominate her to the point where she is like putty in your hands. Yes, everybody knows how to fuck, but the key is to connect with the mental and emotional first. Once you do this, the physical will be over the top. You have to be extraordinary and know how to make her lose her mind. I make a woman hunger for me. I create a longing inside of them. I then help them to realize that the only person who can fill that void is me. And if, for any reason, she feels she does not have a void, I convince her that she does.

See, people have to realize that pimping is basically all about the mouthpiece. It is what you say and how you say it. It is detailing and giving a picture of life, in your own words. It is selling that picture and letting them know that the only way they can obtain that picture is through you.

I create a bridge and let a woman know that once she crosses that bridge, it is no longer about just her. It is now about her seeing us as a team. And, not just any team, but a winning team.

This pimping thing is like running a store. And I am an entrepreneur. When you run a store, you put out your products. The products that sell the best are the ones that the customers want the most.

There is no better product in the world than pussy. Pussy is what makes the world go around. If you have a top-notch hoe, then the customer is going to be willing to pay top notch money. If she is a bottom feeder, then the price is not going to be as much.

Let me ask, how many wars in this world be they big or small, do you think was started in some form or fashion, over a piece of pussy? Men have been killing each other since the dawn of time, over some pussy. They have been bending over backward just for a piece of pussy.

Pussy is like buying a pair of shoes. To get the brand new Jordans or Steph Curry's on the market, you are going to pay top dollar for them. Hell, Nike has this concept down. But, if the shoes are not new, then nobody is going to pay you top dollar for them.

If a hoe is dirty and the pussy stank, then she is not going to bring you any money. This shit is just common sense. Yet, at the same time, a true player in this game is not going to turn down the dollar. He is not going to say no to the dollars that a bottom-feeding hoe is going to drag in.

Unlike most dudes, I do not stick my dick in none of these hoes. It ain't about that. For me, it is always about the dollar. And, I cannot emphasize the following point enough, it is all about the mouthpiece. Yeah, I know that they want me, and I use this to my advantage, but I never lose sight of the fact that it is about the money. I keep feeding them a dream. I let a hoe know that even getting to have a glimpse of this dick, let alone getting to have it, is a privilege.

✖ ✖ ✖

Now with regards to the mothers of my children, my relationship with them was different. We were on a different level than I was on with a hoe that I was pimping. With each one of my baby mothers, there was something to me that was new and attractive. Even with that being said, however, when things went bad between us, they went all the way bad. Yes, we had our ups and downs, just like any couple does. My BM's and I were connected to each other with a level of understanding that what I did, my pimping, was what I did, and completely separate from our own romances, or so I thought.

My first BM, I will not mention any of their names, understood this perfectly at the beginning of our relationship. She knew what I did and was down with it. Hell, there were times when she would even help me pick up women and recruit them into the fold. She would be my point woman and even would spit game to the women for me.

There were times when I would be halfway across the city and she would call me and tell me that she had a bitch waiting for me. When I say that she was down with me, I mean that on every level. Hell, she would even lace them up on how to fuck a man right so to get him hooked.

It is crazy because one minute she was in it with me full force, then the next minute she flipped out on me. That is why I said that a woman's emotions are like a minefield.

She really started tripping out on me. All at once, she decided that she was no longer down with what I did. She acted like what I did was an excuse for me to be fucking with someone else. And, she thought that if that happened, she would end up losing me. She thought that I would no longer have an interest in her.

In no way did she ever stop to think that, or realize that, my dick is not attached to any type of feelings. Hell, the only thing besides my body that it is attached to is money.

See, it is a fact that very few women can actually have sex, and have it on a regular basis, without having their feelings get involved. Most women, some on their first time, get attached and they equate those feelings with love. They automatically assume that the man is experiencing these same feelings. Most of the time, they are dead wrong!

The only women I know who can have sex with a man and actually keep their feelings separated from the act is a hoe. They have mastered the art of simply fucking. Most people can find something negative to say about a hoe, but can't nobody accuse them of being over emotional women that have to cling to a man.

My BM never wanted to share me. And, she wasn't. She was just having a hard time seeing things that way. Because of this, we eventually grew apart.

I can say that she gave me a most precious gift. She gave me my first child. For all of her shortcomings, she is an excellent mother.

✖ ✖ ✖

My second BM was a dream woman. I loved everything about her. It may sound funny, but I also loved everything that she wasn't. By that, I mean, she was not always running around in the streets. She was not a club rat or a party girl that had to be out all day and night. Also, she was the kind of woman who listened to her man. That is a rare thing to find these days. Most women act as if they not only know all of the answers, but that they know the questions even before they are asked. They are stubborn, thick-headed, and act as if they have the world all figured out.

My second BM was faithful to me and had a rare quality of being loyal. There was no doubt that she was committed to me. For me, however, she had one gigantic flaw, she just was not nasty enough for me.

See, there are things that I was accustomed too that she was not doing. She was not showing me that freaky side that I needed. She was not making or keeping our sex life exciting.

Now I am sure that in time, I could have shown her how to fulfill my every need, and she probably would have been interested in learning, but I was not into teaching. I was a very impatient man.

Plus, I was too caught up in the streets and chasing money. I could not put in the time that was needed to cultivate her to my desired taste. I was not about to slow down and miss out on getting my money.

The crazy thing about us is, neither of us actually broke things off. We simply drifted apart. Looking back on it, I can pinpoint the start of our decline to the time her house got shot up one night while we were asleep.

About that night I don't remember much except going to sleep with her beside me. The next thing I know, she was shaking me awake and saying that the house was being attacked. My first thoughts were that she was joking and trying to see if she could scare me; then, I heard the shots for myself. I bolted out of the bed. I could smell in the air the scent of guns having been fired. I do not know exactly how long they shot up the house but it seemed as if it went on for forever. I instantly knew that it was one of my enemies retaliating and trying to catch me slipping.

Once it was over, I was out in the streets. I was looking for some get-back. It was crazy because I could not find anyone. Usually, you would see fools all over the place just hanging out and shooting the shit, but on that night, the streets were like a ghost town. I was already pissed off for being shot at, and not being able to strike back only increased my anger.

My BM called her dad and he came to pick her up. He and I never really got along, and probably never will. He always thought that I was not good enough for his daughter. I did not give a damn about him or his opinions.

It was not long after that incident that she and I sort of drifted apart. I was so caught up in the streets that I did not spend much time with her or the baby. She was fed up and was missing her family. She ended up moving further away and took the baby with her. I just shrugged it off and got myself deeper and deeper into the streets. It became so normal to me that the streets are where I stayed. I kept doing what I do best and I got me another bitch.

There is no doubt in my mind that had things gone a different way between the two of us, she would be here with me right now. She was the type of woman that would ride for me through thick and thin.

I know that she actually hates me right now because I ended up having another baby by someone else. Yet, at the same time, who I am, and the way I carry myself, along with this pimping game I got down to a science, has a hold on her heart that she will never be able to shake, no matter how hard she tries.

She knows that she will never be able to find another man who can even come close to comparing to who I am. I function on a level that is beyond her understanding. I do not yield to the things that most men do.

✖ ✖ ✖

Men are emotional creatures as well. We go through changes just like women do. We have our ups and downs, our good and our bad days. The thing is, a lot of men are just as good as hell at hiding it. I am an expert.

I am a master at both manipulating emotions and getting a woman to see things my way. I can smile in a person's face, pat him on the back and make him think that everything between us is all good while, at the same time, the anger in my heart is growing with each passing second. Homie would never have a clue as to the firestorm brewing inside of me.

I know for a fact that the moment a man just let's go and begins to get all emotional, one of three things happen: first, he gets eaten alive by other men. He becomes a laughing stock. In their eyes, he is a sucka. He is considered a chump. He is labeled as a bitch or a pussy. Everybody starts to treat him like he is as soft as cotton.

Now in response to that, those men usually become even more emotional as they try to defend themselves. They start to lash out and expose themselves to even more ridicule. That is when the cycle repeats itself.

Second, they are looked upon as a pushover. Most women will eat a weak ass man alive. They will run all over him. It will not take long before the roles in the relationship are switched and she will be wearing the pants. She will be calling the shots and controlling the relationship.

And, not only that, she will start talking all crazy to him and lose all form of respect for him. She will start raising her voice and getting all loud and disrespectful toward him. Hell, she might even start putting her hands on him if she deems him weak enough to take it. I know a whole lot of women who are capable of kicking a man's ass if he gives them a chance.

Third, he loses all manner of respect for himself. As far as I am concerned, this is the worst of the three. If, as a man, you have no respect for yourself, then you cannot expect for other people, no matter who they are, to respect you.

Now I know that because I was not willing to become all emotionally caught up with my second BM, she felt as if maybe I did not care about her as much as I did, but that is not true. It is funny because although we speak, we don't actually talk. Now what I mean by that is, whenever I call her, we will speak to each other, but all of our words are shallow and have no deep meaning to them. If I was to ask her how her day has been, we both know that I would not be asking because I cared. I would only be asking just to have something to say. She knows that I really do not give a damn. And, it is vice versa. She does not ask me anything serious because we both know that she could care less. The only serious topic of discussion between the two of us is my daughter. My BM tries to act as if she does not care that I am so invested in my child, but I know that she does.

Hell, there are thousands of men who are not locked up and can provide everything in the world to their children. They can spend quality time and give them all the nurturing in the world that the child needs growing up. Yet, these sorry ass nigga's do not even take advantage of the chances they are given.

I would give anything in the world to be in their shoes. Fuck the bitches, it is all about the kids. They need the guidance. A hoe is going to be a hoe and that is just the way it is.

With that being said, I will say this, I do not in any way, regret my third child, but I definitely regret my third child's BM. She put me through a roller-coaster ride. She was the absolute definition of a computer love.

I met her ass on Instagram. I saw a photo of her and was like, "Damn, I got to have her." She was fine as hell. When I say I had to have her, I mean that I really did have to have her.

She was young, smart, gorgeous, sassy, quick-witted, and most importantly, she was eager to learn. She stayed trying to get in the game. She was always trying to stick by my side when I was out in the streets. She was like a sponge soaking up this pimping game, but by catching this case, I ended up leaving her out there in the world to the wolves. And, like anybody that lay down with dogs, she picked up her

232 EAST OAKLAND TIMES, LLC

own fleas. By that, I mean that she ended up acting like all of those no-good ass hoes out there.

Now, she's a hoe. She won't work. She refuses to get a job. And, whenever life circumstances and being broke force her to get one, she cannot keep it. All she wants to do is sit around on her ass all day, or be out running in the streets. She acts as if she does not have a care in the world.

The worst thing about all of this is, when it comes down to taking care of my child, she acts as if she does not have any form of parental instincts. She is not doing any of the things that a mother is supposed to do to teach a girl how to be a lady. But, I guess I cannot really expect for her to because she does not have a clue as to how a lady is supposed to act. She has never been one.

I know that if it was not for my daughter's grandmother, my daughter would be lost. She would be a wild child. Her grandmother does all of the things for her, that her mother should be doing. Her grandmother is filling in the gaps.

Even though I despise how my BM treats our daughter, the two of us remain cordial. We communicate, and when we do, I try to keep the arguing down to a minimum. I do not hate her, after all, I just do not like her.

I know that in her heart, she would want to get back with me if she had the chance, but I could never see that happening again. I do not go backward when it comes to relationships. Plus, knowing now that she is a hoe, it could never be the same.

As I think about things, I realize that with each one of my BM's, as with most women that I have had in my life, I eventually moved on from them because they started to lie and become manipulative. They all understood my lifestyle and what I was about, but as time went on, each of them became jealous, in their own way. They started wanting more and more of my time. They tried to smother me and force me to choose between them and the other women in my life, or choose between them and pimping. For sure, the pimping won out always.

But, by me knowing how they were thinking, I wound up manipulating them and playing them against each other. For example, one of them might have something that I wanted, so during that time, I would focus my attention on her. I would give her quality time and make her feel as if she was the only one. I would give her a false sense of hope. I caused her to think that she had won me over the others.

Knowing that they were mostly sexually motivated, I would also use this to my advantage. I knew that they wanted me, but that the more I held out, the hungrier they would be and the more eager they would become to satisfy my every need. It was all a matter of playing with their minds.

I also knew that none of them got along with the others so I would stir up the jealousy pot and have them ready to tear at each other's throats in order to have me for themselves. If one of them saw a photo of me on the other's Facebook page, or on Instagram or something like that, they would go into a rage. They would try to outdo the other to win my satisfaction.

While I was out on the streets, I had them in line, but now that I am locked away, for the time being, they do whatever in the hell they want to do. They are at each other's throats on social media. They are talking shit about me and the way that I treated them, yet at the same time, they are each claiming to be the one for me and to be with me.

Since I have been locked up, I have asked them to try and get along if for no other reason than for the sake of my kids. I want my children to know their siblings. Everybody in the world knows the damn saying about a woman being scorned. She will do whatever she has to do to enact revenge in some sort of way. And, that means that she will even use your kids against you if she has too. There is no limit to the ammunition that women will use.

Now there is no doubt that most of the stuff that they are doing they are only getting away with it because I am locked up. If I were out, I would make sure that my kids were around each other every day. They would be spending quality time together.

Each of my BM's told me that they felt betrayed by me because of how I ended up getting my next BM pregnant. I cannot understand it because all of them hoes act like they were not out in the streets doing their own thing. In the end, I know that it does not even matter because they are all out there screwing around with someone else.

✘ ✘ ✘

As I have said before, my kids are my world. My oldest, my son, Lil. O, is my ride or die. When I was out on the streets and doing my thing, I kept him with me as much as possible. He was on the track with me when I was running them hoes. He was riding with me when I was doing my thug thing. And, he was always learning how to be just like his daddy.

I remember the feelings that came over me when he was born. I was in the delivery room and cut the umbilical cord on him. I felt like for the first time in my life, everything was right in the world. When I saw his little face, my heart burst with pride. He looked exactly like me. I felt like no matter what, I had a legacy in him. I had a purpose.

Now I could not verbally express these feelings because, at the time, I did not know how too. Giving voice to the things I was experiencing was not a common occurrence. Hell, nobody in my family ever visibly showed emotions like that. I was never exposed to that sort of thing. And, I know that if I had been, I would have looked upon that person and labeled them as being a soft ass punk.

The crazy thing is, just as soon as those good and happy feeling began to settle into my mind, they were overshadowed by feelings of worry and doubt. I knew that the main thing for me was to now be able to provide for my son. I had to figure out how I could get some money and I had to do it quickly. I was broke and had a new mouth to feed.

I was coming from the bottom of the bottom and had absolutely nothing. I do not think that we even had a can of soup to eat at the time. We had no outside support. I was not working and she had no government assistance. Hell, we were the worst of the worst.

At this point in my life, I was at a real crossroads. I was caught up between thugging and pimping. I was on the fence and had one foot planted on each side.

Now, most people cannot understand this and do not know the difference between the two. Thugging means that I was caught up in the streets. I was actively engaged in the gang life. It was by far, more enticing to me. I was hanging out with my homies, getting high, and smoking weed on a daily basis. I was doing a lot more dirt. I was going out on missions. Hell, I even saw and was there when a lot of my homies got killed.

As crazy as this may sound, there is a lot more appeal to being in this lifestyle than most people would think. That is why there are so many young, black men who are out there grinding in the streets getting their paper and making a name for themselves in their hoods. This lifestyle has an attraction like none other. And, though many of these square' ass dudes in this world will not admit it, they too are enticed by this lifestyle. The world is seduced by the thug lifestyle. If it was not, then why are there so many people emulating the thug lifestyle? Why are there so many movies being made about it? Why are so many songs being written and sung about it? And, why are so many videos being produced depicting the lifestyle?

Women love bad boys. They are turned on by gangstas. They throw themselves at the thugs of the world.

Not only that, but there are far too many men to count that pattern themselves after gangstas. At the same time, there are so many suckas in this world who actively hate on thugs. They will go out of their way to try and throw salt on the game. They are the true definition of the term HATERS.

So, as a thug and having a newborn baby, I had to head out and hit the streets and make me and mines some money like never before. I did whatever I needed to do. I had to provide my son with formula to eat, pampers to put on his ass, and clothes, shoes, and a roof over his head. By doing so, my boy grew up seeing the game first hand. He had a respect for it and he imitated his dad.

I recall a time when I took him to Walmart with me. On that day, I found out how much like his dad he really was. We were walking down one of the aisles and I saw this fine ass woman in front of us. I mean she had an ass big enough to eat off of. She was sexy as hell. Just as we were walking past her, my son put his hand up her skirt and touched her on the butt. She instantly turned around and looked at me, assuming that I had done it. I explained to her that it was my son who had touched her, and she laughed. My son put on this cute, innocent looking face and then smiled. The lady was like putty in his hands. She bent down and gave him a hug and a kiss on the cheek.

I told him, "Boy if you keep this shit up, you are going to have me sent to jail." I was so proud of him. I knew that he had the pimping blood flowing through his veins. He was on track to be a real pimp. I do not think that I could have steered him in any other direction even if I wanted too. From that day forward, I kept him exposed to the game.

Now with my second child, my first daughter, the very first thought that crossed my mind when she was born was that I was going to need a bigger gun than the one that I had. I knew that I was going to have to go all out in protecting her. She was the most beautiful child I had ever seen. I knew that she was coming into an evil world. A world that would have no mercy on her or show any type of weakness. I knew that there were those in this world who would not hesitate to steal the innocence from her life. I was not having it.

Not only did I know that I needed a bigger gun, but I also knew that it was up to me to teach her about the true ways of the world. While other people were allowing their kids to live in a fantasy, I knew I had to give her the real so that she would not fall for the bullshit that was sure to come.

Also, I knew that she needed someone in her life that could teach her how to be a little lady. Her mother was perfect for that. She would definitely steer my daughter in the right direction. My only worry in that was that I did not want my daughter to become dependent on a man for any reason.

Now lastly, with regards to my third child, my second daughter, I was not on the streets when she was born. In turn, that made me feel like I needed not only a bigger gun, but two bigger guns. I regret that I missed out on her birth. I know that I need my freedom to be able to protect her. I am hurting every day that I am not there to fulfill my duties as a father. I cannot say much about her because I am behind these bars and the loss I feel by not being in her life is a heavyweight that I carry each and every day. I want more than anything to get out there and show all of my children that their father is down for them.

38 YEARS LATER

ROBBERY KIDNAP

1

UPBRINGING

P eople take much in life for granted. Usually, we overlook the
simplest of things: the smell of fresh cut grass, a home-cooked
meal, the comfort a dog can bring, relaxing at a beach and hearing the
ocean roar.

Life's simple pleasures are what I gave away. What do I mean by
that? I am the only person in my family that has been to prison. I
cannot attribute it to my upbringing. My older sister had a small run-
in with the law due to check and credit card fraud. She ended up
with probation. My life surely wasn't predestined to be this way,
locked up for generations. Often, I look back, in reflection, to understand how my life took this turn. My Name is Brian Shipp and I and
currently incarcerated at San Quentin State Prison for the crime of
kidnap robbery. I am in my 38th year of a 7-to-life sentence. This is
the story of how I got here.

I was born in Alameda California in 1958 to a loving mother and
father. Alameda was a Navy town off the San Francisco Bay. We
lived in a charming three-bedroom home. The home had a large backyard and a fireplace. It was a different world back then. The country

had wrapped up the conflict in Korea. There were beginning talks of "make love, not war."

My dad worked as a barber. He was very good at his craft. Many of his customers had been coming back to him since the day he set up his chair. My mom was the typical housewife. Her daily tasks were to cook meals and keep the house clean. Despite the help that women gave us in WWII, the notion of women working seemed still a futuristic thought. It was uncommon for women to get equal pay as men back then.

My older sister and brother are four and eight years apart from me. When I look back at that time of my life, we were very close. I can't remember any fights we had back then. I could go to anyone in my family and ask for almost anything. Most of my childhood was blessed. I was happy and had plenty of friends.

✖ ✖ ✖

At my age of four, we moved 25 miles inland to Alamo California. The move marked the first significant shift in our way of life. My dad had always talked about opening his own shop. He could make a lot more money if he didn't have to pay a percentage to a barbershop owner for renting a barber chair. As a result, my dad bought his own shop where he set up business. It was his way of being independent and not work in someone else's barber shop. He wanted the American dream and to provide for his family.

Business was a little slow as he started off. Most of his customers were back in Alameda. It took a lot of word of mouth to actually get him out of the red and into the green. The new business was a highly stressful enterprise.

I guess the new stress took its toll on my mother and father's relationship. Shortly afterward they separated. While my parents were separated, my siblings and I tried to carry on as usual. It has never truly dawned on me the impact their marital problems probably had on my life.

My parents lived in separate homes. I assume they hoped to rekindle their love but sometimes when people separate they understand just how far apart they are. Couples often find that both may love the other, but they both want different things in life. My parents divorced a few months later. Their divorce was a shock to me. I was under the impression that they were just fighting and would soon make up.

Next came the decision of whether they should split the kids up or let us remain together. I guess they figured they would give us the choice. All of us siblings elected to stay with our mom. This may have been because dad was the disciplinarian. He was also usually gone when we came home from school. Mom was the voice of care and regard.

We spent weekends with our dad. He also would come by and pick us all up on Monday after we got home from school. Being able to see him on Mondays was special. He would take us to his apartment. It was a small one bedroom but cozy apartment. There we all had chores to do. He never used to do any chores as he would make reference to chores as women's work, so we cleaned. Us kids made his apartment immaculate.

My dad's friends seemed to warm up to us quickly also. Some of the persons that would come by my dad's were family members, distant aunts, uncles, and cousins. We would go to Shasta Lake with my dad and his friends. Most of the people that went to Shasta Lake went to party. I'm not saying my dad's intentions weren't to party, but he welcomed and watched over us. Our stay was usually a week long. It was a great vacation. We would ski and hike and sit around bonfires at night. We made smores before they were a household name.

The vacation would come to an end quickly. My dad would take us back to mom's place. I could see her smile as we pulled up. Then I guess a thought would overtake her and she would look at the ground as we exited the car. My dad would wait just long enough for us to close the doors to the car. With a short wave, he would drive away. At my mom's we sat around and watched TV.

My sister had an estranged relationship with our dad. They seemed to fight all the time. Maybe it was his way of parenting or his way of showing love. My mom really only wanted us to be happy and have fun with our lives. I think it was a phase that my sister and dad were going through. Nothing outrageous, just the typical father and daughter bickering. Nevertheless, their fighting would upset me because I wanted all of my family to get along. Despite me being the youngest, I felt as if I were the nucleus for harmony in the household.

My brother and I have an eight-year age difference. I looked up to him and was basically his shadow. He really didn't like when I would tag along with him. When I would bring up to mom my brother's resistance, she would tell him to take me with him. Most of the times we fought about that. If we weren't fighting, he would stick his finger in front of me and tell me to bite it. I would do so and he would thump me until I let go.

One time my brother woke me up in the middle of the night and told me to hurry and get ready for school. I got dressed as quickly as I could and ran outside. It was pitch black. He locked the door and would not let me back in. Nothing to intentionally hurt me, just annoying. He found ways to agitate me for his amusement. By doing so, I think he had hopes of me not following him around. Despite these types of conflicts, I still got along well with all of my family.

✖ ✖ ✖

I don't think my mom anticipated the great struggles of being a single parent nor the cost associated with being a single parent.

Mom did the best she could to provide for and raise us. We lived like nomads moving between dwellings in Alamo and Danville, California. We had a limited income coming in. My mom worked as a waitress in various diners. She also received money from child support paid by my dad. Much of the diner work was temporary or at least felt like it to me. The sad part was that bills didn't wait for her to get another job. She eventually filed for welfare and food stamps. We couldn't make it without assistance.

All of the places we lived in were dilapidated. If the houses had back and front yards, the yards were full of weeds. Weeds left little or no spaces for me to play. The weeds could be as tall as me. Sometimes, there were holes in the walls from the punches or kicks of former occupants. I guess the property owner never cared to repair them before re-renting the places. I pretty much accepted the fact that these were the type of living quarters that mom could afford at the time. My main concern was having fun. I tried to accomplish that with as little parental supervision as possible. Mom wasn't a disciplinarian. She would only inflict her wrath if we disrespected her or each other.

Despite our financial straits, I was still relatively happy. I actually enjoyed growing up in various neighborhoods. I was outgoing and made friends quickly. Older people seemed to warm up to me and enjoy my company. If I was a bother to them, they never let me know. I held in my mind a belief that adults hold a fountain of knowledge. I would ask questions about any and everything to pick their brains. Nevertheless, it seemed as soon as I settled in my mom had plans to move again.

My mom started dating. She was an attractive woman and would be good for any man. She met a guy named Jack. They started seeing each other on a regular basis. I guess they both felt the relationship was going in the right direction, so we all moved in together. We moved to a bigger home in a town 30 miles north of Danville called

Pittsburgh. The home was beautiful and had a yard full of green grass. We would play slip-in-slide on hot days in the backyard.

I can remember coming home one day and my mom had a smile on her face as big as Texas. She announced to everyone that we would have an addition to the family. She was pregnant. Jack seemed genuinely happy also. We all liked Jack. He would take us out shopping and buy us any toy we wanted. He kept us in new clothes for school or church. He had a convertible car. None of us had ridden in one before. He would let the top down and we would drive everywhere and let the sun warm our faces and the wind whip through our hair. Our favorite place to go on warm nights was Baskin-N-Robbins. I loved their ice cream. Jack would also take us to the Santa Cruz Boardwalk. He would pay for us to go on all the rides there. Our days would end with swimming in the Pacific Ocean.

I was enrolled in a new school. I didn't know anyone in the town or at the school but I didn't let it bother me. I was a likable person and people warmed up to me quickly. I was getting used to starting over. All schools seemed to have the same curriculum, so each time I started over I fell right in and wasn't left behind. I had a passion for math and music; I was a natural at both.

✖ ✖ ✖

When I was around 10 years old, I got a job working for the United California Bank. The work consisted mostly of cleaning up the parking lot and maintaining the foliage. At least once a week I pulled the weeds in the parking lot. I also trimmed the hedges. I loved the smell of fresh juniper when I cut it. I used the money to open a checking and savings account at the bank. The savings account would grow with each paycheck. In addition to the landscape maintenance job at the bank, I created flyers advertising lawn care for families that were on vacation. The slogan on all the flyers was, "Your lawn and plants will be greener and healthier when you come back from your two-week vacation!"

I was 12 years old the first time I bought my parents and siblings Christmas presents. It felt good and I continued to do so every year. This was done regardless of whether I had a lot or little money. I made sure everyone in the family had a Christmas gift.

I started playing the drums around 10 years of age. I wanted to be just like Mikey Dolan of the popular band, "The Monkeys." My friends and I played at the 6th-grade graduation. The performance was in the auditorium at the school. We were a hit. All the girls were screaming and yelling. I played a drum solo at the end. It was a song from Iron Butterfly called, "In-A-Gadda-Da-Vida." The crowd went wild. I really felt like a superstar. I was very popular in elementary school and paired up with the prettiest girl.

In the 7th grade I excelled in school. I took advanced Algebra classes. I also grasped Geometry and statistics. I enjoyed math. It was a great time of life. I was nominated for best dressed and finished in second place. These sorts of accomplishments made my parents proud of me. Despite of all the good I was doing, I also had a dark side.

2

_____

CRIMINAL THINKING

M y first misdeeds were relatively small. I began shoplifting in
local stores. My first impulse to do so was around the age of
10. I took things that we needed at home from the grocery store or the
local Five & Dime. I felt an immense rush from shoplifting. There
was a great thrill experienced each time I walked out of a store
unnoticed.

Once, I got caught stealing from the the local Gemco department
store. The security staff snatched me up while I exited. They banned
me from that store, which, honestly, wasn't enough of a deterrent for
me against future stealing. I continued to shoplift, but I did not do so
day in and day out. I changed my tactics into a new scheme. I would
switch the price tag on an item in the store and then pay for it. Basically, I would find expensive brands and then switch the price tags
with cheaper brands. I would then go to male cashiers because most
men weren't familiar with the items. Later in life, I pulled the same
scheme in automotive stores. In automotive stores, I would go the
female cashiers as most of the women cashiers knew less about car
parts. Not once did I ever have a problem or any suspicions from the

stores and I did this on many occasions. Nonetheless, it wasn't enough. My idiotic criminal thinking would talk me into greater misdeeds. My head always had me thinking the grass greener on the other side, that a quick score would put me ahead. I was adamant against the poverty mind frame: in other words, accepting a life without what others had. I smoked my first joint around this time as well.

My criminality evolved into the burglary game. A friend and I broke into homes. First, I would knock on the door and hide, similar to the door knock game kids play. When we were sure no one was home, my friend and I would go around to the backyard and look through the windows. We preferred homes with doggy doors as the doggy door gave us a means for easy entry. On my belly, I was just small enough to crawl in a house through the doggy door flap. My friend would hold up my legs so I could fit in. Once inside I crept around the house to make sure no one was present. My heart would beat a mile a minute. I would then go to the back door and let my buddy in. We wouldn't ransack the house. All we took was food and alcohol. I never took any valuables, such as jewelry. We did this three times in three different homes.

My buddies and I would also take cars on joyrides. People often would keep their extra keys either balanced on the visor or under the floor mat. The first car we stole was a Fiat 850 Spider. We drove the car to the Cow Palace Arena in Daly City for a New Year's Eve concert. We were both 13 at the time.

3

7TH GRADE

In the 7th grade, my vision took a turn for the worse. I began wearing glasses. Also, my dad required me to wear dress clothes. My teeth were crooked and I wore braces. I was no longer the cute kid. I was now a weird looking glasses and braces monster. To add insult to injury, I had wild crazy hair. I became a type of outcast. I pulled away from the friends I had. I started spending most of my weekends with my older sister. She married when she was 16 years old. In those days, it was more common to marry that young. She's four years older than me. It was cool hanging out with my sister and her friends. My brother-in-law kept my mind occupied as well. He got me started helping him work on low-rider cars. We would often go to the junkyard looking for used parts we could salvage. It was a lot cheaper than going to the store to purchase them.

My brother-in-law and his friends didn't care what I looked like. There were welcoming of me for I was a curious and fun kid who was always ready to help out or join in on an adventure. Since those days, I have had a passion for cars.

4

COMING OF AGE

I value all my friendships and have always been a devoted friend. I'm a genuine person and would give myself or money to help others. If we were going somewhere, I would pay their way to help them enjoy the occasion. I have always been a good listener. My heart nor my character has ever been out to deceive or cheat a friend. I would go out of my way to be there; this is just what friends do. I honestly enjoy the act of giving. People would classify me as shy at first, but when they got to know me, they would be attracted to my heart and character.

✖ ✖ ✖

I was without a peer group and wanted to be accepted. I grew my hair long and stopped wearing the dress clothes my dad bought me. I began buying my own clothes. By purchasing my own clothes, my dad couldn't tell me what to wear. My attire was jeans and hiking boots. I also wore long sleeve Pendleton shirts, even on hot days.

Due to boredom and being shy, I experimented with drugs. I used drugs to take the edge off and for conversation. At that time, I wasn't addicted.

One of my connections for psychedelic mushrooms, "shrooms," was considered a "Dead Head." He and his friends loved the Grateful Dead and went to every concert that was performed in the Bay area. After hanging out with them for a while, I found new acceptance. My new friends and I would go on hikes up mountainsides. We would camp out on weekends and smoke weed. A number of us played instruments. One guy played the bagpipes and my best friend played guitar. We would sit around campfires singing along like we were a commune. The pretty dead head girls and dudes all got along well. They all hooked up except me. I was liked for my personality. At the time, I was a follower of these friends. Before I was a leader. It was an ugly stage of my life.

✖ ✖ ✖

I got my driver's license and purchased my first car. It was a 1966 Pontiac Bonneville that I quickly turned into a low rider. I was the only guy in my high school with a low rider. I used to get a lot of attention when I pulled up. Interestingly enough, at school, there was also a lady with a low rider.

Daily, I would spend hours working on my Pontiac. My brother-in-law's cars were my inspiration. I needed stylish tires and rims and a booming stereo.

The great thing about my Bonneville was that it was large enough to carry all my friends. We would all pile in and go to keggers or house parties. I never tried to race my car.

✖ ✖ ✖

I, like most teens, rebelled against any and everybody. I had quarrels with all of my teachers. My woodshop teacher was cool, though not tolerant of weed. One day, I smoked a joint before going to class. He asked for my assistance with grading papers. I didn't think twice about going into his closed office and grading papers. When he walked in, he frowned. I looked up with a confused look on my face, trying to gauge his feelings. He said, "Learn to wear cologne. You reek of weed." I gave him a look as if I didn't know what he was talking about. He then added, "You'll ruin your life smoking that crap." I respected this teacher and wanted to listen, but as I said, I was in my rebellion stage and let his words of wisdom drift in one ear and out the other.

At age sixteen, I got a job as busboy in a local hotel. I have always been a diligent worker, so I quickly worked my way up to the title of lead man. The lead man position brought more steady work and longer hours. I worked overtime as much as possible. I wanted more money. I also sold lids of weed at school to earn money. A lid was the term used for an ounce. I would throw smoke out parties. People would buy my product and have a good time. Selling pot helped my income.

Selling weed was a lot easier to do at parties that the jocks threw. You would think that jocks would be clean and sober. Quite the contrary. Jocks were my best customers. A lid of weed cost fifteen dollars. Selling weed was a good income supplement. I was making around an extra $30 a day selling lids.

One day while standing in front of an apartment complex waiting for a customer the cops swarmed on me. I had four lids of weed, which amounted to a quarter pound. I didn't have time to hide it or stash it. They patted me down and found the pot. I was taken downtown to the police station. Since I was a minor, they called my dad. He came and I was released into his custody. They gave me a $200 fine to pay. Since it was under a pound, I received a misdemeanor. I was put on restriction for a month. Restriction was like a prison to me. I was used to being outside working and having fun, but now I was stuck in the house all day. I didn't feel like the punishment was just. I was seventeen years old.

✗ ✗ ✗

I found my first love during my senior year at Del Valle high school in Walnut Creek, California. Our classes were next to each other, so I would see her in the halls. Although I lacked the gift of gab, I ended up sparking a conversation with her. We hit it off immediately. It was as if I knew this woman my whole life. We could talk about anything and everything. Our shared interests brought us closer together. We were both athletes and loved the outdoors. However, when we talked about family, we were opposites. Her family was wealthy and offered her support in whatever she did. My broken home saddened her and made her feel empathetic towards me.

As our relationship progressed I proposed to her and she accepted. We were engaged. Things seemed perfect, but we lacked maturity. Plus, this beautiful woman loved attention. She would flirt with people all the time. Sometimes even in front of me. I didn't believe myself to be smart or handsome enough to possess such a beautiful woman, which led to me being jealous of her and her flirtatious ways. Eventually, we separated.

✗ ✗ ✗

I was feeling down and out. I needed to do something to take my mind off of my ex-girlfriend. My friends and I decided to throw a kegger. My dad was away on vacation. He left me in charge of the house. We had a huge party. Everyone that was anyone was there. I don't know how they found out, but kids from all over Contra Costa county showed up. Music echoed throughout the house and beer flowed like water. Everyone had a great time, drinking and dancing. There were many pretty ladies. I brought cocaine. Lines were shared. I felt like a celebrity. The party was a hit. I had another kegger party when my dad went on his second vacation.

✖ ✖ ✖

Those were great and spontaneous days. I tried black beauties and cross tops, types of amphetamines, when I wanted to stay awake. I also tried acid hits in different forms but never really enjoyed the high.

I remember my first acid trip. I was at a party at a friend's house. Everyone there was on it. These guys were messing with a girl who was really high. She was having a bad trip. Somehow, she managed to climb up a tree and was stuck. She was scared and kept calling for me to get her down. I was frying so hard I couldn't move to help her. All I could do was watch. I never felt so helpless. I knew that drug wasn't for me.

5

_____

INDEPENDENT

B y age 20, I lived a good life with a beautiful girlfriend. I wore nice clothes and rented a stylish home in Walnut Creek, an upper-middle-class area. I furnished the home with high end household items. I left no expense spared. I purchased all Maytag appliances. The stove was huge. I prepared lavish meals for breakfast and dinner. In the freezer, I could store almost 20 pounds of meat. My living room set was the talk of all my friends. When I threw get-togethers, everyone had plenty of room to sit on the plush sofas. For my lady friend and I, my king size bed offered us a spacious oasis. Finally, I owned two vehicles. My Monte Carlo was my pride and joy. I also had a new Honda 750 Supersport bike. Riding motorcycles was my hobby. I would put on my boots and jacket, gloves and helmet and go. I loved the feeling of the raw power of the bike between my legs.

I learned from the start to put everything I could in my name, my lease, phone, etc. By doing so, I would establish credit. From working at the bank I learned how having a credit record was an upcoming mean to financial success.

The braces were finally removed as my teeth were now straight. Looking at myself in the mirror without a mouth full of metal made me smile. I clipped off the long curly hair and wore my hair short, combing it back. The last time I had my hair cut short was a punishment after I got caught with pot by the police. I didn't like short hair back then, maybe because my hair was cut despite how I felt. I also upgraded from glasses to contact lenses. Contacts were new and innovative. The first couple of times inserting the contacts required perseverance. My natural impulse was to close my eye as my finger approached. I had to force my eyes open until I got the hang of it.

Now looking at myself, short hair, contacts, and a metal-free mouth, I felt like a new man. With my new look came new confidence. I was back being the natural born leader. I asserted myself in conversations, when before I played the silent role. I had more influence over my friends. I was growing into adulthood.

6

WORK LIFE

I was working a warehouse job. My co-worker and I got along well. We were making scraps compared to what I knew the job was worth. We talked a few times about our wages, or I should say we vented about our wages. Everything was above ground until he told me a scheme. The scheme involved us manipulating the invoice manifest. It wasn't rocket science, all I needed to do was get a blank invoice slip and rewrite the quantities for parts ordered. I tried rewriting an invoice but got caught the first time. I didn't count on each invoice slip being numbered. I guess this was for tracking and billing purposes. When I turned in my slip to the office, it was logged with one number that fell out of sequence with the previous number and the following number. I don't know entirely, but they did find the discrepancy. The supervisor immediately called me in for a meeting. I was asked to explain the difference. Of course, I couldn't. I was terminated based on my actions.

I liked working with my hands. I couldn't see myself sitting in a cubicle all day. I loved the outdoors and the sun too much. I started a landscaping job. My Dad told me that it was seasonal work and I should look for another job. I did.

The second warehouse job I had was for a large linoleum company. Most of it was menial work. I unloaded trucks and had light inventory duties. I got raises on a regular basis. These types of jobs left little room for advancement and the money, regardless of raises, was peanuts.

The money wasn't enough so my criminal mindset in. I got fired for stealing. Again, I was hoping to live more comfortably and get some extra money. Due to thoughts of having bigger and better things, I would take unnecessary risks. All in all, I was okay financially and really didn't need to take such risks, yet criminal acts merely seemed easier and faster.

I look at myself as being a hustler. What I mean is that I will create a revenue source. I have always put my all into every job I ever worked. I made impressions on most of my employers. Good standing helped me to quickly move up in the rat race. With some jobs, I had opportunities to become a salesman but as with the linoleum job, trying to do something underhanded ruined excellent opportunities.

Home life wasn't a factor in my criminality. As I said I'm the only family member that has come to prison. My ambitiousness and desiring of nice things led to my criminal activities. I think in a way I disappointed my family.

7

JOYRIDING

One day while out with a friend, I took a 450 SL Mercedes Benz that was parked next to my 1978 Monte Carlo. I had wanted a Mercedes since I was knee-high to a grasshopper. My friend and I just had a great breakfast at Copper Skillet, in Dublin, California. I loved their hash browns and country fried steak. The car door to the Mercedes was unlocked. I opened the door and flipped down the visor looking for the keys. No luck. Something told me to check under the front seat. Sure enough, the keys were there. I immediately told my buddy to follow me, throwing him the keys to my Monte Carlo. He followed me and parked my car in another parking lot. We headed out to San Francisco.

I loved to go to San Francisco because it was a beautiful city, a city filled with trendsetters and diversity. My favorite spot to go was Fisherman's Wharf. People from all over the world visited Fisherman's Wharf. You could sample every kind of cuisine imaginable. The drive takes 45 minutes. I obeyed all speeding laws on the way. The last thing we wanted to do was bring attention to ourselves. We picked up three girls. It was a little weird because they were dressed like mimes.

We hung out for a while walking up and down Fisherman Wharf. The weather changed and it started to get cold and windy. Such weather is common near the San Francisco Bay. It was time to go home. The girls seemed to have a good time hanging out with us. I asked the girls if they would give us a ride back. I flatly told them that car they had been riding in was stolen and we planned to leave it in San Francisco. They didn't believe me at first, but once they saw us wiping the car down for fingerprints, they knew we were honest. They agreed once we promised dinner. Turns out they were country girls from the outskirts of the Bay Area. It was a fun time.

8

SMALL BUSINESS OWNER

I was always good at working with wood. In school, I was an assistant to the woodshop instructor. One of my friends knew of a construction job working for an associate of his. I worked with this associate building a redwood deck. The house where we installed the deck was lavish. I burned to have enough money to buy a home, especially a similar high-end home.

We only had one job. When finished, this new work partner and I had no other jobs lined up. We sat around for a week doing nothing. I thought we could get more work with the right advertisement. I said, "I know how to get work. But we will be partners now." We called ourselves B&B construction, given that another company had a similar name so we thought the name similarity would help us. Neither of us had a business or contractor's license. Nonetheless, we went and printed business cards and flyers. I placed the flyers in mailboxes. Basically, I put flyers anywhere I felt customers may be found. I had to get our name out on the street. A most vital part of any business is advertising.

About three days after our advertising blitz the phone started ringing and jobs began to roll in. Soon, I didn't have time to handle the phones and be out on the job at the same time. I had to hire an answering service to handle all the calls our business was getting.

I separated from most of the people I knew in high school. For a time, I associated with one buddy from my younger years. In school, we had a very close bond. However, I needed to end that friendship. He and his girlfriend were selling cocaine. I wanted no part of that scene and the people it brought. I was working on making B&B a success. I developed friendships with more law-abiding business minded people. These new friends had their lives in order and seemed to be going in the right direction. We were all successful and equal. No one was a leader so to speak, but all had value to offer the others.

✖ ✖ ✖

Poverty shaped me. Growing up I was not ashamed of living off food stamps or the government housing that was provided to my mother and us. Still, I never wanted to be on government assistance or receive food stamps for myself. I have always strived to be a successful man. My need to accumulate money stemmed from my impoverished upbringing. I have a need for bigger and better things. This need would consume me and take over my thought patterns. I created various endeavors to build income. Acquiring money became my preoccupation. I put gathering it before further schooling or college. I sought another paycheck or additional cash from marijuana sales. Selling marijuana was the one gig I always kept.

_____

SPA INSTALLATION JOB

You know the old saying that time flies when you're having fun. Well, that's true when running a successful business. I was in my second year of business. The jobs kept rolling in and I felt accomplished in life. My work schedule was rigorous, often 16 hours a day and always seven days a week. Such hours were required to complete the numerous contracts we secured. I had thoughts of hiring additional employees to help cover the workload, but finances wouldn't allow the expense. With company overhead, we remained in the red. Most profits were spent on tools, equipment, vehicle upkeep, etc. Nevertheless, running a company felt great.

Everything changed after I signed on for a spa installation job. The client commended us on the craftsmanship and detail we put into the job. He also admired our work ethic and character. In particular, he felt I was an upright person and he offered to buy into the business. He said that he knew many people with wealth and he could convince them to hire us. He would use his gorgeous spa as an example of our work. The man's wealth was evident to us and the

terms favorable, so we agreed. I couldn't see much wrong with
the deal.

He called a short while later informing me that he acquired a spa
installation job in Danville, my old hometown. He set up a meeting
with the client at the client's business in Dublin, a neighboring city.
We met up without incident and signed all the necessary agreements.
One clause of the contracts requires clients to pay for half of the job
upfront. The clause was our insurance against buyer's remorse. I had
to safeguard my purchase of materials. We learned of the need for
this "insurance" the hard way, through struggles to get money from
clients. As we met in this new client's Dublin office, the conversation
and interaction were going fine. The client was reading through the
contract. He stopped while reading over the paperwork and stated,
"You know I don't have to pay you at the completion of the job?" I
thought the statement odd and was taken aback. In reading through
the agreement, he realized that our business operated without proper
licensing. I wanted the job and I wanted to move forward with the
signing. I replied, "Yes sir that is correct. I have you sign this form and
I perform my job to high standards. After the job's completion, the
next thing for you to do is pay me for the services." He then offered to
use his own contractor's license number. Using his license felt like a
safe bet so I agreed. The client asked one of his employees to bring
the contractor license to us. After a few minutes, the employee came
back without the license as he couldn't find it. The new client looked
disgruntled. He then stated that if I could come up with two thousand dollars, he would help me get a license from Sacramento. I
declined that deal in an instant. I didn't have that sort of money to get
a license that had doubtful benefit to me. He told me when I did have
the money to phone him and he would walk me through the licensing
procedure. We started his job the next day.

The entire time I worked on installing the client's new spa, what he
said about not having to pay me resonated through my head. I feared
he would not pay us. I distrusted and disliked the man. I felt there

was something tricky about him. I deliberated on the reasons why they couldn't come up with his contractor license number. The license should have been on multiple forms and letterheads. The man had me worried I was digging my own grave.

After completion of the job, he paid me with a check. I preferred cash and before each job requested cash from all clients. I submitted the check for deposit. It did not clear. When I called the bank to inquire what was the holdup, the bank notified me that the checking account the check was written from was opened up with funds from a personal check and that personal check had a 30-day hold on it. I had to wait the same amount of time for the check to clear. It felt like a slap in the face. These types of unnecessary complications are why I always requested cash. I felt like the client was purposely delaying my payment, deliberately screwing with me.

10

BLACK JACK LUCK

The check finally cleared. I breathed a sigh of relief. I felt like I beat the guy. I received the $1100. Luck was on my side. My construction partner and I decided to take a trip to Lake Tahoe to gamble.

On the drive up, all I could think about was how much money I was going to win. The way my luck was going, blackjack was my ticket to fast riches. I had been playing blackjack in casinos since I turned 18 years old. Even though we had the $1100, things were tight financially. I, personally, needed some extra money until we finished a Gazebo job we had.

Black Jack, a.k.a. 21, was the easiest game to play and win. I hit the tables and sat on the third chair looking toward the other players sitting near me. I wanted to gauge what type of players I faced. Not too long into gambling, my partner lost all the money he had, $550. I couldn't believe it. Now I felt like I had to win for both of us.

It was around 2 p.m. on a Saturday afternoon. I sat at that table for hours. The momentum shifted back and forth from the dealer to us gambling at the table. I would hit some good runs and stack a few hundred; however, I couldn't reach my goal of $1400.

By 9 a.m. Sunday morning, I was out of money. The house is bound to win I suppose after that amount of time at a table. I walked off with my head toward the ground. The walk of shame. I know many have taken it before me. I had no money whatsoever. I nothing left for gas or for a meal. I looked through the car hoping I had stashed some money somewhere. To my luck, I had my business checks safe in the dash compartment. Even though checks weren't accepted at most of the places, we were able to find a meal. At the self-service gas station, I filled up and handed the cashier a check. The clerk refused at first but I had no cash so he had to accept the alternative of taking the check. We then hit the road and headed home.

The next day I went to work thinking of the predicament I was now in. I didn't have enough money to complete the contracts at hand. These new financial straits were the last thing I needed. I begin to put my focus on the spa client who issued me a time-delayed check. I felt anger at his way of addressing me regarding my not having a license. I thought him arrogant and that he put unnecessary burdens on others. He never paid any interest for the wait time on his check to clear. Thinking about this client made me more irate by the minute. Slowly the thought of everything that had gone wrong in my life pointed towards him, his arrogance and his wealth. I decided to rob the client. Of course, I understand now I was irrational in my attributions of guilt.

The client had two five-gallon water jugs full of money sitting next to his fireplace. They were full of bills and coins. He noticed me staring at them while at his home so he explained the intent of the jugs. The client and the client's son were jointly saving money to buy the son his first car, once the son turned 16. As an adult, I had never robbed anyone. As a kid, as mentioned, I broke into a few homes but I hadn't tried such a thing as an adult. I didn't care about of the good intention to be had with the jugs of money. In fact, frustrating that purpose may have egged on my own desire to have the coins for myself. I decided to rob this client's house of those coins.

11

MY CRIME - FEBRUARY 13, 1980

I went over the plan with my co-worker. It would be a quick in and out job. All we wanted to do was grab the jugs and split. He thought it was a good idea also. We decided guns would be needed in case there was any trouble. I have never shot anyone, nor planned on doing so. The only time I had shot a gun was skeet shooting with neighbors while younger. I had a buddy that had a few firearms so I called him to borrow a couple. Luckily, he didn't ask too many questions. He loaned me a .22 caliber rifle and a .38 caliber Smith & Wesson pistol. The guns had no ammo so I went to Gemco to buy bullets. Later, I also purchased nylon stockings and beanie hats, gloves and rope. I wanted to be prepared for every contingency. Little did I know the surprises ahead.

I was restless the night before with thoughts about our plan. I finally dozed off to sleep. Tuesday arrived. It was February 13, 1980. It was the day of the heist. I woke up before the break of dawn. There was a gazebo installation job to complete and I was scheduled to meet with potential clients later in the day.

Both of the day's tasks went well. I installed a lattice on the gazebo and I secured a new job to build a deck. The new clients even paid me half the money on the spot. Walking out of their home, I knew I was now free to walk into the former client's home and proceed to rob it. I hoped to knock on the door, just like I did as a kid, and after finding no one home, simply enter the house and walk out with the 5-gallon jugs filled with coins and cash. Yet Murphy's Law, that whatever can go wrong will, manifested itself in full force that Tuesday evening.

I had no other vehicle, so we decided to use the company truck. Driving the truck left us at a disadvantage. Even though we didn't have any branding on the truck, the guy knew the vehicle. We parked the truck on a dirt road next to the Danville fire department. The road was about a block and a half away from the guy's house.

I sat in the truck for a few minutes sweating. My first thoughts were to call it off, but I kept getting pissed by what the client put us through. We decided it was time. We were all set with our nylon stocking face masks. We wore the beanies to cover our heads. We also wore turtleneck sweaters. All that could be seen of us was our eyes. Everything we wore was expendable. We had intentions to burn all the clothing afterward. Neither of us had a record, but we wore gloves just in case.

There was not a lot of traffic in the area. We didn't think it necessary to hide the firearms, so we walked with the guns in hand. I had the rifle and my partner had the .38 special and rope. He also carried a buck knife in his belt to cut the rope. Our plan was to be prepared for anything. It took us only a few minutes to reach the house.

The first thing I did was cut the phone line. There would be no calling for help on my watch. As we started toward the house, a station wagon pulled into the driveway. A man and woman were in the car. I had never seen the pair before. My partner and I looked at each other. Although we didn't speak, we seemed to agree that things were going wrong from the start. We paused for a moment looking at each other. I motioned for us to leave. He seemed to think about it and finally shook his head no. How different my life would have been if we did leave.

Now, we knew there were definitely people at the house, people we didn't count on being there. Further, we understood, if guests were arriving there also would be hosts. While these thoughts flooded my mind, we met a greater surprise, four people appeared from the side of the house and faced us. My partner reacted quickly. In a threatening voice, he yelled for them to not move and get back into the house. I then popped up. I shouted in a disguised voice for them to get back into the house. They all complied immediately.

We entered the house with the four in front of us. There were two men and two women. My partner made the two men lay on the carpet in the family room. He tied their hands behind their backs. The ladies were told to sit at the dinner table and not move. My heart was pounding a million beats a second. Out of the corner of my eye, I noticed a kid in the house. He was told to not move and stay seated on the couch. I stood there with my rifle drawn and made sure no one moved. One of the ladies sitting at the table looked at me. She kept peering at me even though all she could see was my eyes. She looked at me intently as if she knew me. She then asked, "How did you get yourself into a predicament like this." I sort of felt she was sincere, but there I stood, nonetheless, looking like a terrorist. I replied in a confident filled voice of intimidation, "Easy!"

My partner searched out the house. Within seconds he returned shaken and startled. "The house is surrounded," he yelled. "There are cops everywhere. They got floodlights on every window!" "How the hell could there be cops here?" I replied. We weren't in the house for more than a couple of minutes. That news was a shock to me.

I quickly ran to a window and looked outside. I pulled the curtain back slowly. I was blinded by the floodlights. I promptly shut the curtain and tried to regain my vision. I then ran back to the dining room. My partner stood there motionless. His lips quivered as he asked, "What are we going to do?" Neither of us had planned for any of this occurring. I was no robber and these types of plots were never explained in TV shows yet there was nothing else to do except plan our exit. I said, "We're getting out of here." I pulled up one of the men from the floor and motioned for my partner to grab someone. I thought we would get away if we could make it back to the truck. Two persons volunteered to go with us. The police were notorious for shooting people back then so the plan was to use the people as human shields. I told my partner to stay in the house and I was going to pull the parked car in the driveway closer so my partner could exit with the additional hostage. He agreed. I had no idea who the man was I held tight to me but I knew the police weren't playing around. We exited the house. My gun was in hand. I didn't want to hurt him but I had no intention of allowing the police to shoot me. Plus, my mind was set on not giving myself up. I had no intention of going to jail and I thought I would get away.

Everything seemed to move in slow motion as I walked outside with the man as hostage. Everywhere I looked were police. Their flood-lights shined directly in my face and covered every inch of the house. My partner was still in the house. I hoped he wouldn't do anything stupid. From the driver's side, I pushed the guy into the station wagon and over and into the passenger seat. I got into the driver's seat. The car was in the driveway but I wanted it closer so my partner could jump in. I started the car and inched up the driveway to a spot beneath the awning. My partner saw me and quickly exited the house with a female hostage in tow. He jumped into the back seat with her and I began backing the car out of the driveway. Suddenly, it was as if a fourth of July celebration began. Explosions started going off. Bullets rained in on us. Glass from the exploding car windows was flying into our faces and all around us. The sounds were deafening as percussion grenades exploded. Why were they shooting at us? I yelled, "Everyone get down!" As I said that, I felt a sharp pain in my arm. I lowered my head as much as I could while still controlling the vehicle. I could tell they were shooting at me and I was surprised. I only had intentions of getting away. I continued to see explosions and gun barrels burst in front of me as we drove down the street. We reached a cul-de-sac so I swerved the car into a chained gate hoping that I could gain exit that way. The station wagon easily proceeded through the chained gate. The car bumped around through the grassy field of a school. I bounced around in the car trying to maintain control of it while looking for way to exit the school field. The guy that sat next to me yelled, "Did you get hit?" He seemed to repeat this question over and over as I didn't respond to him. I had to stay focused on the terrain in front of me. I could tell he was sincere with his concern. The car seemed to swerve left and right. They had shot out the tires on the car so it was extremely difficult maintaining control. I didn't know the area or school I was driving through. I kept asking the guy next to me, "Can I get out this way?" He responded, "I don't think so." I drove as far around one of the building as I could searching for an exit but there was none to be found. The tires were shot out on the car. The rim started to dig into the grass now. We were going nowhere fast. The car slowed to a crawl. I still had not given up hope of an escape. I put the car in park and jumped out. I left the rifle on the front seat. I hopped over a fence and ran towards a vacant lot. I heard shots being fired at me. Bullets seemed to whiz just inches above my head. Some of the bullets were so close I could feel the wind as they passed. What I didn't know was the entire time my partner had been shooting at the officers. I yelled at him, "Get down now!" as I realized we were in the crossfire between two groups of police. When my partner stopped shooting, everything became eerily silent. I wondered if I was dead. The ache in my arm told me I was alive. My heart was pounding and I was soaked with sweat and blood. Realizing I was shot increased my panic. The surrounding area was covered with the sight of flashlight beams. I saw I had gone the right way and the company truck was within sight.

My partner crawled on his belly toward me and we crawled in the direction of a stack of tractor tires piled on top of each other. We climbed inside. The police had brought in dogs. I hoped that they thought we had fled and they would continue on looking for us elsewhere. It seemed like an eternity that we sat there waiting for them to leave. However, the cops didn't leave, they only got closer. I heard the dog handler say, "Come on boy, find 'em." I never saw the dog but eventually, lights flowed into the tires like they were transparent. I heard the officer say, "Get out slowly with your hands up." Raising our hands, we both climbed out of the tires. We were slammed to the ground and handcuffed.

I was placed in the back of a squad car. I had a gunshot wound to my left arm. While sitting in the car, another officer covered in mud ordered the driver to shine his light down on me. The second officer pointed his hand at me as if his hand was a pistol. He then pulled an invisible trigger while making a shooting noise. He shouted, "You bastards tried to kill me!" His pant leg seemed to have a bullet hole in it. The assumption being that the hole happened when my partner was shooting in their direction. They cut off the light and slammed the door.

I was transported to the hospital and treated for my wounds. The nurse described the gunshot wound as "through and through." It only needed to be cleaned and sutured. I was handcuffed to the bed. A group of police officers stood by as the medical staff attended to my injuries. A cast was put on my left arm. The cast ran from my armpit down to my wrist. I was chained to the hospital bed at both ankles.

My dad was granted permission by a judge to see me while I was in the hospital. That was the worse feeling of my life. I was discharged from the hospital after four days.

✖ ✖ ✖

I feel my arrest was a blessing and a curse. A blessing because I'm still alive. A curse because of where I have been for the past 38 years. What prompted the police to come as quickly as they did was a combination of my having cut the phone line to the house and the homeowners having had set up security systems due to previous burglaries. I guess God has funny ways of preventing us from doing further damage in life.

12

FREE ON BAIL

I was processed and booked into the station jail. I was assigned a court-appointed attorney for representation. He came to the substation to visit with me. The attorney was skeptical of my chances against the charges. He listed them off:

Count 1: Kidnap for the purpose of robbery

Count 2: Attempted murder on a peace officer

Count 3: Robbery with use of a gun

The charge of attempted murder had no grounds. The attempted murder was based on the officer who had a small caliber bullet hole in the leg of his trousers. The assertion was either my partner or I shot him. I believe with the number of shots the officers took, the bullet was from one of their guns.

My bail was set at $87,000. I had no way of paying that kind of money up front, even if I took out loans and borrowed from everyone I knew. Two days later I went for arraignment at municipal court. The judge noted that it was my first offense and I wasn't a flight risk.

He reduced my bail to $20,000, which was still a huge sum of money but I thought I could gather it. I felt it would be easier for me to fight the charges from the streets rather than from prison. I began making calls.

There weren't many people in my life I could go to for money. I had one close friend from high school who did have some money and I made a deal with him to work in exchange for bail help. This kind-hearted person agreed to loan me a majority of the $20,000. The rest of the funds were gathered from everyone I knew.

I made bail. I was glad to be free. I worked on weekends at my friends' ranch. It was light and simple work, but I did these menial tasks with a smile on my face.

I continued to work as a carpenter and did various handyman tasks to keep an income coming in. The court dates seemed to be scheduled every three months which gave me plenty of time to live. It was a back and forth battle between the multiple motions my lawyer and the D.A. seemed to file against each other. I honestly had no defense. From what the D.A. said it was the easiest slam dunk case he ever had. We basically were caught red-handed with hostages in tow. The hope was to resolve the charges via a plea-bargain.

13

MARRIAGE PROPOSAL

I had a lot of crushes on TV stars growing up. I loved Jaclyn Smith; her role on Charlie's Angel's brought many smiles to my nights. There was also Brook Shields. Her overall persona attracted me. In the real world, I can only think of four women that captivated me. With each one of them, I felt I had true love. I asked each of them for their hand in marriage.

While out on bail and I met a new woman. She was only 18 while I was 22. We had a lot in common. I was living at the house of the friend that bailed me out. She would come over often to visit. She was a wonderful lady. At the time, she was enrolled at U.C. Berkeley. Together we enjoyed athletics, such as working out and water skiing. We played tennis and often would play with her parents at a local racquet club.

After a few months of dating, she moved in with me. Yet the ultimate nightmare arrived. I had to go back to jail. She didn't miss a visit. It was a breath of fresh air seeing her, despite the situation. She gave me hope for the future and my new life. I felt with every ounce of me that this was my soul mate.

280 EAST OAKLAND TIMES, LLC

I ended up taking a plea bargain for 7 to life. It was a "decent deal," said my lawyer. My girlfriend was in court and waved at me. It gave me reassurance that I did not have to face everything alone. I was eager to get the court process over. The plea was conditioned on the district attorney dropping the attempted murder and attempted assault on a peace officer charges. I felt those two charges were the most serious and my lawyer agreed. I took that plea bargain in October 1980. My lawyer sold it to me with the hope of me getting out after seven years. Here we are 38 years later and I still fight for my freedom.

When I was a young man, I committed the only felony of my life, which resulted in a 7-to-life sentence for the crime of kidnap robbery. I feel up until that point I was a law-abiding citizen. I was in pursuit of the American dream. I have always felt I am a genuine and an authentic man. I am an honest, compassionate, loving, and very trust-worthy person. My friends, family, and associates have always been able to count on me for anything. I have been there mentally and financially to support all those involved in my life. My prayers are for another chance at life. I feel I have wasted many years in prison that I could have used to make a positive difference in the world. Here I sit 38 years later as a result of one bad decision.

I sat waiting in the county jail for about a month before being trans-ferred. I arrived at San Quentin reception. My girlfriend filled out the visiting form and was approved. On the first visit from my girl-friend, I proposed to her and she accepted my hand in marriage. We were to have a jailhouse wedding.

Part of the marriage protocol required her to write a letter on why she wanted to marry me and to state the reason for my incarceration. A lot of convicts lie about their sentence and the time remaining on their sentence so the corrections department requires would be mates to write a detailed understanding of their loved one's offenses. The letter was supposed to be sent to my prison counselor, but it mistakenly came to me. I read the beautiful letter she had written. I felt a sincere and genuine expression of love clearly communicated in her words. I was at a loss and felt unworthy of such a wonderful person. I loved this woman with every ounce of me.

I began to think that it would be unfair of me to ask her to put life on hold for an uncertain duration of time while I languished in prison. I was contemplating one of the hardest decisions I would have to make in my life. In the end, because of the uncertainty of my sentence, I decided not to marry her. She objected and we fought over my decision. Our correspondence dwindled over the next years. Eventually, she was out of my life.

14

MEETING MY WIFE

I had a friend that worked at Longs Drugs. I asked her if she would create a flyer for me as I was seeking a pen-pal. I sent her a photo I had taken on the lower yard at San Quentin State Prison. I hoped I would get many responses. Before she could put the flyer up her co-worker saw the photo. Her co-worker was adamant that the flyer didn't go up. She would become my pen-pal.

In her first letter to me, she relayed how she had told our mutual friend, "You're not putting this up in the lunch room. I'm going to write him!" Things progressed in our letter writing, so we set up a visiting date. I had a buddy that worked in the visiting room. He had a table reserved for us. He placed a vase with two roses that I had cut earlier from the San Quentin Garden Chapel, a religious meeting chapel at the prison. Our first visit was on December 24th, 1983. Our visit went as well as possible. She began to come to the prison every weekend. We talked to each other about why I was in prison and the potentiality of how long I could be here. She fully understood my situation and had no objections.

15

MARRIED LIFE

I felt in my heart that I was ready and had found the one. I proposed to her with no reserve. She accepted my hand in marriage and the wedding date was set. I then contacted the Family Visiting coordinator and informed her of my upcoming wedding. I hoped to secure a family visit date that coincided with our wedding. I wanted the consummation of the marriage to play out similar to a free person's wedding.

Our wedding occurred in the non-contact visiting area. The same area is now used for the reception of new inmates at San Quentin. KRON News, a local TV station in the Bay Area, wanted to do a segment on jailhouse weddings. They contacted the San Quentin's Public Information Officer and asked if they could film a wedding. They were granted permission to do so. Our wedding just happened to coincide with the time of the filming. We were asked if we would allow KRON to film our marriage. We agreed and signed the waivers. It was actually a good idea because our kids and grandkids could watch it for years to come. The news crew went to my fiancé's home and asked her questions about our relationship. The news crew was also allowed in prison. They shot b-roll of me working at the print shop. They filmed me going in and out of my West Block housing unit and cell. Crazy enough, they were granted permission to take footage from the gun rail above. From, the gun rail they took a long distance shot of my soon-to-be bride driving her van up to the family visiting cottage. The final shot was of my now wife and I, entering the family visiting cottage together.

We married in June of 1984. By the end of 1985, we were contemplating bringing a child into the world. Because we were both raised in broken homes, we had a dilemma. We did not want the same for our future children. She and I had plenty of talks about staying together no matter what. I thought it best to wait until I was out of prison for children. I wanted to be there every step of the way. Unfortunately, prison wouldn't allow it.

After we were together for about a year and a half, we found out that my wife was pregnant. I am a firm believer that everyone should go through parenting school before bringing a child into the world. A tremendous amount of dedication and finances are required to raise a child.

Our first son was born on December 10, 1986. He was beautiful. Now, the pressure of parenting by proxy was at hand. The weekly visiting schedule helped and the family visits, which happened once every three months, helped out a lot. Family visits allowed me three days of family time and bonding. I tried to make it a vacation for my wife. I did all the chores and I cooked all the meals. Cooking has always been a passion of mine. I also changed the diapers every chance I could. I welcomed the challenge, the opportunity to be helpful.

Our second son, an equally handsome boy, was born on June 28, 1990. Family visits were a lifesaver and weekend visits allowed for continued bonding and also socializing with others. Families would stop by and congratulate us. They would comment on how handsome our sons were. On one occasion while changing my son in the visiting room, he let out a burst of urine. The saying is true, "When you got to go, you got to go." It was one of the funniest moments I can remember. So, I learned to ask him when I heard his stomach rumble, "Did you poo, or was that gas?" With the most innocent of looks, he would reply, "gas."

Our family visits were far and few between but I looked at it as a time to bond with my sons. Family visits would allow my wife to see me interact with my sons. Some of my heartfelt moments were when my sons helped me cook in the kitchen. They would handle the small details, like toss scraps or retrieving items from the fridge, with an adorable zeal. I remember my oldest said to me, "Dad I like your cooking."

My youngest was around a year old, the day of our last family visit. On that day, my boys and I awoke before mom and played. I fed my son a bottle. My wife awoke around 10 a.m. I cooked my wife her favorite breakfast, the same breakfast I would cook for her each visit, Eggs Benedict.

By 10 p.m., while feeding my youngest a bottle and listening to my wife, I passed out. I was either nudged by my wife or just re-awaken. She asked me if I was going to listen to her. I was exhausted. I realized I was tired after a day with the children on a mere family visit. I considered the magnitude of what my wife must go through daily.

16

SAN FRANCISCO CABLE CARS

I did the best I could to send money to the family. I was fortunate to end up in a prison that had a hobby shop. The hobby shop is a place where you can order materials to do woodwork. I started making miniature cable cars, modeled from the cable cars in San Francisco. I also made miniature pianos and jewelry boxes. I created three different size cable cars which sold primarily at the hobby store at San Quentin State prison. With the business mind I have always possessed, I hired three inmates that had no outside financial support and no woodworking experience. They were good, diligent men that simply made a mistake and wound up in prison. Each man assembled and glued the cable cars. As a result, I was able to send a minimum of $200 a month home to my wife. During the holiday season, I would gross $1000 a month. My miniature cable cars enabled me to help my wife purchase Christmas presents for the kids. Even though I was incarcerated, as a man and husband I still felt I had a duty to provide for my family. I feel I was the best lover, father, and friend possible despite my prison incarceration handicap. In fact, through our dual efforts, in 1986, we were able to save enough money to buy a home.

Despite being in prison, I was transforming my life into that of a successful man.

17

DIVORCE

B y 1991, I could tell that my wife was tired of the routine. Something just didn't seem the same during our visits. She sat right in front of me, but I still felt distant from her. I loved her with all my heart, so I was at a loss. Prison can wear the best of us down. It wasn't designed to hold families together but tear them apart. Neither of us was to blame, but divorce was on the horizon. I thought a good way to show my wife that I loved her was to allow her to live her life. I wanted her to be free from the prison confines of my life. That way my kids could have a father there with them every night instead of just weekends. It was indeed the hardest decision I had to make in my life. It would, in fact, deny my part in the lives of my boys. My oldest son was about four at the time. My youngest was just rounding a year old.

I explained the situation to my immediate family. Some didn't understand, but divorce was what I felt was right. I reached out to my Dad and my friends to ask each to help support my children. I asked them to bring my children to visit with me from time to time. This was done so my wife wouldn't have to see the pain on my face that divorce was causing me. The divorce finalized that same year.

My friends and Dad helped for a short period of time with visits, but that ended in 1993. No one had the time to bring my kids up to see me. It was a devastating period in my life. I wrote the boys on a regular basis but could only hope that they got my letters. Up to this day, I have never stopped writing to them nor sending gifts.

18

LOSS OF HOPE

Drug use was not prominent in my life, especially at the time of my crime. Yes, I used, but my usage was more so a holiday from life's routine. On the streets, I was not addicted to any drug. I sold marijuana and, at times, other drugs, but I never allowed drugs to grab hold of me. In prison, it was the same. I was more into body-building and working out. Exercise was my greatest stress reliever. I worked out six days a week until in 1998, the year California Department of Corrections decided to remove the weights. At the time, then-Governor Wilson during a tour of prisons saw the shape inmates were in. After the tour, he made a press statement to the notion that prison bred caged animals. His guards stood no chance of defending themselves against such beasts. The positive effects for inmates of weightlifting were twisted and sullied out of fear. He signed an order to remove weights from prison.

At first, the state placed a limit on how much weight we could use. To be able to work out, the state also required the viewing of weight training instructional videos. Finally, correctional officials systematically removed all weights from prisons. Having a stress reliever in weightlifting was sufficient, so drug use wasn't on my mind. Also, I had a day job assigned to me by the prison. I didn't want to miss any time or money, so I hunkered down and pursued my business as a stress reliever.

I had my life in order. I went to my scheduled progress hearing. The Parole Board found me suitable to be released into society. Everyone was excited, including me. During this period, the governor can revoke your parole grant for basically whatever reason he deems. This was a terrifying period for me due to no lifer, at that time, ever clearing the governor's signature. We were called "political prisoners." As it happened, the governor denied my parole.

I lost hope as a result. I felt powerless. I honestly thought that I would never see society or home. I began using drugs for comfort and, eventually, spiraled into misery and started heavy drug use. I called my family and friends and told them I was never coming home. I told both not to write to me anymore, and, by then, I was no longer contacting them. I slowly became a drug addict.

19

DRUGS AND TVS

During this period life was overwhelming. Crack and meth use was a daily thing for me. To make matters worse, I was just getting out of Administrative Segregation, the hole, after four months. I had been charged with "Conspiracy to Commit Bodily Injury to a Correctional Officer." That was a serious offense. Apparently, a black prison gang called 415 had plans to commit the act. I honestly had nothing to do with the conspiracy. Nor did I have a residue of knowledge about the plot yet I had to endure the entire disciplinary process. Prison staff was to investigate the likelihood of my participation. Please know that in prison, you're guilty until proven innocent.

Meanwhile, I was in a cell 23 hours a day. Eventually, the pain ended. I was cleared of the rules violation and, without an apology, released back to the mainline.

Now everything I had accomplished was gone. By being in the hole, I lost my prison job and my hobby shop woodwork enterprise. I needed a new income source. Prison offers opportunities for revenue, either legal or illegal. I chose the legal realm. I knew a guy that had a few TVs stocked up. I propositioned him to buy the TVs at a discounted price. I slowly began to buy 13-inch color TVs and rent them out to other inmates. All the enterprise required was for me to keep an inventory of how many TVs were rented out, to whom the TVs were rented out, and the balance owed to me by each renter. I had a monthly rental fee of two cans of Bugler tobacco. Cans of tobacco sold for $5 at this time. At my peak, I owned and rented out 22 13-inch TVs. I acquired that many TVs in one year.

The TV repairman had 16-inch color TVs that he wanted me to rent out for him. He didn't like dealing with inmates because of the games they played. I agreed to do so. I also needed his help to maintain my own TVs. Thus, with the additional 16-inch TVs, I was renting approximately 38 TVs on a monthly basis.

The income was great. I was profiting on average 60 cans of Bugler at $5 a can so basically a $300 monthly cycle. I still needed to expand. I created a T.V. guide business and had 145 customers. They each paid a pouch of Bugler a month, which cost $1.45. The T.V. guide business brought in revenue of $210 a month. From both endeavors, I was making $510 a month.

The TV enterprise was how I supported myself and my ever-growing crack and meth habit. I understood I should have been sending the money home, but drugs had me. I couldn't wait to get back to my cell to get high. There were small clusters of inmates lined up outside my cell waiting on me. They knew my money was good. I would easily spend a couple hundred a week getting high.

20

DRUG TRANSPORT

I nmates are either bussed here or arrive in a van, as San Quentin is a Northern California reception center. San Quentin also serves to house general population inmates and holds the men on California's Death Row.

The inmates that were lined up outside my cell generally had some connection to the reception inmates. The reception inmates came directly from the county jails or other prisons. Drugs were clandestinely transported by reception inmates to San Quentin. New batches of prisoners came through Monday through Friday, yet drug contraband arriving with them was never guaranteed. There were days when nothing came in. We called those "dry days." Dry days happened mostly on weekends when no new arrivals pulled up.

Dealing with my addiction was rough during those dry periods. The quality of the crack and meth also varied. Some of the stuff was really good; other times you got crap. I had various connections to ensure that I got the best. Of course, I had inmates who had their old ladies bring drugs in through the visiting room also. I did everything under the sun to get high.

21

FUNCTIONING ADDICT FOR JESUS

I had no goals or cares at this time. My mental state was focused on my total destruction at any cost. If I died from a drug overdose, it would be an end to my misery. I used crack and meth on a daily basis which made my tolerance grow. I hoped I would use so much that my brain would explode. By overdosing, I would not have to suffer or endure the pain of prison anymore. I thought about my family every time I got high. The pain of separation and not seeing them made me delve deeper into usage. I was a full-blown addict and could care less if I died. I would have full week runs of getting high all day, every day. I would use until my body gave out and crashed.

At that time, I classified myself as a functioning addict. No matter how I felt, I still got up and went to work. The psychosis part about my addiction was, I would applaud myself as to how I could maintain responsibilities while high. I continued this drug-induced state until a couple months into 2002. The only thing that stopped me was being a drummer in the church. I felt I was disrespecting my Lord and Savior by coming to church loaded. I was representing the church while the drugs were coursing through my veins. There was a sermon one week in which I felt God was talking directly to me. The preacher said, "Whatever you might do outside of this church is your own business. But remember, outside you all represent the body of this church and not just yourself." I took that to heart and had to step down from the church with hopes of getting my life together.

Shortly after stepping down from the church I was approached by a correctional officer while at work. The C.O. told me I was being placed into Administrative Segregation for suspicion of giving an order to have an inmate jumped. Allegedly the inmate who was jumped was a snitch.

Here again, I found myself in the hole pending investigation. I stayed there until I was transferred to Old Folsom State Prison in 2002. It goes without saying, but while in Administrative Segregation I was drug-free. Additionally, the transfer to Old Folsom from San Quentin helped to maintain my sobriety. I was sober for almost a year.

During this time, my mother passed. I received a share of the family mineral rights. The value of my inheritance was around $7700. My plan was to pay off my debts. I chose to give my two sons $500 each. I owed my sister $1500, so I paid her off in full. I paid my best friend $500 for the filing of a writ, a legal petition. The writ was an appeal filed against the Board of Prison terms for denying my parole date. Sadly, I blew the rest of the money on drugs and quarterly packages. Drugs had called me and told me they were my friend.

Whenever I would go on a drug binge, it seemed I would I find myself in Administrative Segregation. I was placed in the hole again. This time for another conspiracy charge. I was there for seven months. The blessing was I was able to re-establish my relationship with my Lord and Savior Jesus Christ. I studied the scriptures daily. I would wake my day up with God's word and wisdom. I shared my Daily Bread, In Touch, and Discovery Bible Reading Guide with the other inmates there. It seems that most of us in the hole were lost and needed spiritual guidance.

Despite being locked in a cell for almost 24 hours each day. I found the peace that I was seeking. I had peace and joy in my life and heart for the first time in decades. This time when I was released back to the mainline I continued my relationship with God and not the drugs. I began seminary classes through Golden Gate Baptist Theological Seminary School. Our church had arranged all the paperwork to facilitate these classes. The church offered any inmate who desired to learn about our Lord an avenue to do so through college courses.

Study and prayer helped me tremendously. I worked on my fellowship with the Lord each and every day. I was growing stronger in my relationship with God. But I was still weak. I watched a friend do a shot of meth. I was weak in fighting my addiction and in not more than two hours I had a needle in my arm. The rush came back and all that I had gained seemed to be lost. I didn't leave my cell for three weeks. All I could muster up to do was go to chow and the shower. I was just chasing the high of meth. I was lucky I didn't lose my job as a result. I would call in sick every day instead of reporting in. I lied and told my supervisor I had the Norovirus. The Norovirus makes you have diarrhea and vomiting at the same time. It's highly contagious and had been going around the prison. My supervisor didn't think twice about me not coming in. I would do one big shot each night after the guards secured the lock bar and the tier was clear. I would do this for many nights straight until my body would shut down.

Today, I am an usher at the Protestant chapel at San Quentin. I love the church. Occasionally, I fill in on the drums for the "praise and worship" ceremony held for reception inmates.

I started going to different classes and programs offered at the prison. I enrolled in another college called Patten University. My goal was to earn a second A.A. degree; my first being a theology degree. I studied hard and earned A grades on my tests and papers. I love to read. I believe reading more has helped my grades and my mind.

I also am a drummer in a prison band. We play all sorts of music from rock and roll, rhythm and blues, and even classical. Our performances occur in the yard. Music is a way to help me get my life together.

22

LOVE AND HUMAN KINDNESS

Thoughts of staying drug-free for my family gave me strength. My ex-wife and I hadn't spoken in years. My relationship with the kids was estranged. My youngest didn't want anything to do with me. The boys ended up being raised by a step-dad. I tried everything possible to be involved in their lives. I send letters constantly as well as gifts when I can afford the expense. I know such items are not the same as fatherly love and parenting but I, at least, want the boys to know I always think of them.

In 2005, I was blessed with a letter from my boy's mother. She wanted to bring the kids to the prison for a visit. She wanted the boys in my life and I in theirs. It was the kindest thing anyone has done for me while I have been in prison. The boys and I had a wonderful visit. It was very emotional seeing them after all the years. I remember sweating profusely before the visit. It felt like I was seeing them for the first time. I received some flak and anger from my youngest boy. He was very upset that I was still in prison. He, of course, has a right to be. Children need their father at home. There was no excuse nor did I try to create an excuse for my absence. He told me, "If you put my brother and me first in your life, you would've been out by now!" I took that to heart and have done all I can since then to come home. I was blessed with a grandson by my oldest son in 2016. I am very proud of the job my ex-wife did raising our children. Both of them have excelled in life. They both have college degrees. They have blossomed into outstanding men. I am very proud of them. I thank God for shining his light on them. The good outcome of their lives has shown me that a rose can grow through concrete.

From the time of my divorce, I rejected all outside female contact. I didn't want to start a relationship with a woman. I was afraid of hurting another woman emotionally like I did my first wife. It wasn't until a few years ago that I agreed to correspond with someone. Through our writing, we have grown very close. We are now planning to get married. This marriage will last the duration of my days on earth. She is a beacon of hope for me. I hope to be released soon. I will spend the rest of my days thanking her for making me whole again.

23

LIFE LOOKING IN THE MIRROR

My life took a tragic turn from a terrible decision. It was one day and one moment in time. I have so much regret and empathy for the family I robbed. I have empathy for the officer almost injured in the events of that day. I keep them and their families in my prayers. If you take anything from my story, please realize that it only takes a split second to throw your life away.

I have learned to be proud of the man I see in the mirror. I do wonder what I could have been, but I prefer to look at the steps in life I have made. I'm a recovering addict. Without the trials and tribulations, I have endured I would be less of a man than I am today and am destined to be. I am a recovering addict who has by God's grace found acceptance of who I am and what I have been.

I am studying business for my release. I imagine myself getting a real estate license and flipping houses or perhaps obtaining a wholesale license to sell cars. I studied Spanish for the past few years as I see the demographics of the country change. I feel knowing a second language will only be a benefit. I possess a solid work ethic and I know how to prioritize my responsibilities first. My father instilled this work ethic in me. He never missed a day of work. Whether he was sick or just burnt out, he still rolled out of bed and did his job.

I hope this story will have a positive effect on you. I ask that you stop and think before making any rash choices. Our choices can have never predicted or conceived of ripple effects. These effects can reach into the lives of future generations, your own kin, community, and not to mention your own life. I pray you can live vicariously through my life without making the same mistake.

EAST OAKLAND TIMES, LLC

The East Oakland Times, LLC (EOT) is a multi-media publication based in the San Francisco Bay Area. Founded by chief editor, Tio MacDonald. EOT has at its core three principles: the principle of the dignity of life, the principle of liberty, and the principle of tolerance. EOT supports the flourishing of civilization through the peace found by honoring these three stated principles.

Current Projects Include:

• Publishing of the My Crime Series

• The Publication of Original Inmate Art and Books

• Podcasts from California's Condemned Row

• Quarterly Print Publication for Free Distribution on the Streets of East Oakland

• Website Dedicated to Inmate Reporting on Current Events

Please remember by leaving a review you encourage others to buy the books in the My Crime series and thereby YOU support EOT's mission.

For exciting My Crime series bonus materials, such as interviews of the subjects of the series, go to www.crimebios.com

Support the EOT by purchasing EOT produced e-books, print books, and audiobooks!

Stay positive & productive!

Unity in purpose!

Tio MacDonald

East Oakland Times

Chief Editor